PRAISE FOR RACHEL

"There is nothing blurry or muted about Cusk's literary vision or her prose . . . She is one of the smartest writers alive."
—Heidi Julavits, *The New York Times Book Review*

"[Cusk] has that ability, unique to the great performers in every art form, to hold one rapt from the moment she appears . . . A stark, modern, adamantine new skyscraper on the literary horizon."
—Dwight Garner, *The New York Times*

"In her effort to expose the illusions of both fiction and life, [Cusk] may have discovered the most genuine way to write a novel today."
—Ruth Franklin, *The Atlantic*

"Cusk has glimpsed the central truth of modern life . . . She moves through it as a blasted centre full only of instinct and superhuman hearing and hackles."
—Patricia Lockwood, *London Review of Books*

"Cusk, like the best artists, has renovated her work from its deepest interior—the self—transforming her private crises into an expansive aesthetic vision."
—Meghan O'Gieblyn, *The New York Times Book Review*

"Quietly staggering and intellectually entrancing . . . [Cusk's] writing is silvery and precise, navigated by elegant syntax that steers its speaker toward revelations of great depth."
—Martha Schabas, *The Globe and Mail* (Toronto)

"[The Outline trilogy] can now be appreciated—and will surely be looked back on—as one of the literary masterpieces of our time."
—Sebastian Smee, *The Washington Post*

"[Cusk] commandeers reality . . . An object lesson in rigor, elegance, and fury." —Merve Emre, *Harper's Magazine*

"Cusk's prose . . . is a tight guitar string or a wire from an espalier. Her descriptions . . . have a bewildering precision, a feeling of painful truthfulness." —Claire Jarvis, *Bookforum*

"Cusk's brilliantly reasoned argument against the false security of narrative continues to hit a nerve." —Megan O'Grady, *Vogue*

"Alienating yet intimate, dreamlike yet grounded, slim yet substantial, delicate but fierce, Cusk's writing feels, exhilaratingly, unlike any other fiction being written these days."
—Emily Donaldson, *Toronto Star*

"[Cusk] writes like someone who has been burned and has reacted not with self-censorship but with a doubling-down on clarity. She is blazingly intelligent, a deep, tough-minded thinker . . . at once freewheeling and exquisitely precise." —Heller McAlpin, NPR

Siemon Scamell-Katz

RACHEL CUSK

AFTERMATH

Rachel Cusk is the author of the Outline trilogy, the memoirs *A Life's Work* and *Aftermath*, and several other works of fiction and nonfiction. She is a Guggenheim Fellow. She lives in Paris.

ALSO BY RACHEL CUSK

FICTION

Second Place
Kudos
Transit
Outline
The Bradshaw Variations
Arlington Park
In the Fold
The Lucky Ones
The Country Life
The Temporary
Saving Agnes

NONFICTION

Coventry
The Last Supper: A Summer in Italy
A Life's Work: On Becoming a Mother

AFTERMATH

ON MARRIAGE AND

SEPARATION

RACHEL CUSK

PICADOR

FARRAR, STRAUS AND GIROUX
NEW YORK

Picador

120 Broadway, New York 10271

Printed in the United States of America

Originally published in 2012 by Faber and Faber Limited, Great Britain

Published in the United States in 2012 by Farrar, Straus and Giroux

First Picador paperback edition, 2013

Picador paperback reissue edition, 2021

The Library of Congress has cataloged the Farrar, Straus and Giroux
hardcover edition as follows:

Cusk, Rachel, 1967–

Aftermath : on marriage and separation / Rachel Cusk.

  p. cm.

ISBN 978-0-374-10213-5

  1. Cusk, Rachel, 1967– —Marriage. 2. Cusk, Rachel, 1967– —Divorce.
3. Authors, English—20th century—Biography. 4. Marriage—Psychological
aspects. 5. Divorce—Psychological aspects. I. Title.

PR6053.U825Z46 2012

823'.914—dc23

[B]

                                                        2012003807

Picador Paperback ISBN: 978-1-250-82829-3

Designed by Jonathan D. Lippincott

To RCJ, wise soldier

Zeus has led us on to know,
the Helmsman lays it down as law
that we must suffer, suffer into truth.
We cannot sleep, and drop by drop at the heart
the pain of pain remembered comes again,
and we resist, but ripeness comes as well.
From the gods enthroned on the awesome rowing-bench
there comes a violent love.

—Aeschylus, *Oresteia*

CONTENTS

AFTERMATH 3

EXTRACTION 29

COUPLES 43

DARK WINDOWS 61

AREN'T YOU HAVING ANY? 75

THE RAZOR'S EDGE 93

XYZ 111

TRAINS 125

Acknowledgements 147

AFTERMATH

AFTERMATH

Recently my husband and I separated, and over the course of a few weeks the life that we'd made broke apart, like a jigsaw dismantled into a heap of broken-edged pieces.

Sometimes the matrix of a jigsaw is undetectable in the assembled picture; there are champion jigsaw-makers who pride themselves on such things, but mostly you can tell. The light falls on the surface indentations – it's only from far away that the image seems complete. My younger daughter likes doing jigsaws. The older one does not: she builds card houses in whose environs everyone must remain silent and still. I see in these activities differing attempts to exert control, but I am struck too by the proof they provide that there is more than one way of being patient, and that intolerance can take many forms. My daughters take these variations in temperament a little too seriously. Each resents the opposing tendency in the other: in fact, I would almost say that they pursue their separate activities as a form of argument. An argument is only an emergency of self-definition, after all. And I've wondered from time to time whether it is one of the pitfalls of modern family life, with its relentless jollity, its entirely unfounded optimism, its reliance not on God or economics but on the principle of love, that it fails

to recognise – and to take precautions against – the human need
for war.

'The new reality' was a phrase that kept coming up in those
early weeks: people used it to describe my situation, as though it
might represent a kind of progress. But it was in fact a regression:
the gears of life had gone into reverse. All at once we were moving
not forwards but backwards, back into chaos, into history and pre-
history, back to the beginnings of things and then further back to
the time before those things began. A plate falls to the floor: the
new reality is that it is broken. I had to get used to the new reality.
My two young daughters had to get used to the new reality. But
the new reality, as far as I could see, was only something broken.
It had been created and for years it had served its purpose, but in
pieces – unless they could be glued back together – it was good for
nothing at all.

My husband believed that I had treated him monstrously. This
belief of his couldn't be shaken: his whole world depended on it.
It was his story, and lately I have come to hate stories. If someone
were to ask me what disaster this was that had befallen my life, I
might ask if they wanted the story or the truth. I might say, by way
of explanation, that an important vow of obedience was broken. I
might explain that when I write a novel wrong, eventually it breaks
down and stops and won't be written any more, and I have to go
back and look for the flaws in its design. The problem usually lies
in the relationship between the story and the truth. The story has to
obey the truth, to represent it, like clothes represent the body. The
closer the cut, the more pleasing the effect. Unclothed, truth can be
vulnerable, ungainly, shocking. Over-dressed it becomes a lie. For
me, life's difficulty has generally lain in the attempt to reconcile

these two, like the child of divorce tries to reconcile its parents. My own children do that, forcing my husband's hand into mine when we're all together. They're trying to make the story true again, or to make the truth untrue. I'm happy enough to hold his hand, but my husband doesn't like it. It's bad form – and form is important in stories. Everything that was formless in our life together now belongs to me. So it doesn't trouble me, doesn't bother me to hold his hand.

After a while time stopped going backwards. Even so, we had regressed quite a long way. In those few weeks we had undone everything that led to the moment of our separation; we had undone history itself. There was nothing left to be dismantled, except the children, and that would require the intervention of science. But we were before science: we had gone back to something like seventh-century Britain, before the advent of nationhood. England was in those days a country of compartments: I remember, at school, looking at a map of the early medieval heptarchy and feeling a kind of consternation at its diffusity, its lack of centralised power, its absence of king and capital city and institution. Instead there were merely regions whose names – Mercia, Wessex – fell effeminately on the ears, and whose ceaseless squabblings and small, laborious losses and gains seemed to lack a driving, unifying force that I might, had I cared to think about it, have identified as masculine.

Our history teacher, Mrs Lewis, was a woman of size and grace, a type of elephant-ballerina in whom the principles of bulk and femininity fought a war of escalation. The early medieval was her period: she had studied at Oxford, and now here she was in the classroom of our mediocre Catholic girls' school, encased in a succession of beige tailored outfits with co-ordinating heels from which it seemed her mighty pink form could one day startlingly emerge,

like a statue from its dust sheets. The other thing we knew about
her, from her name, was that she was married. But how these different aspects of Mrs Lewis connected we had no idea. She gave great
consideration to Offa of Mercia, in whose vision of a unified England the first thrust of male ambition can be detected, and whose
massive earthwork, Offa's Dyke, still stands as a reminder that division is also an aspect of unification, that one way of defining what
you are is to define what you are not. And indeed historians have
never been able to agree on the question of whether the dyke was
built to repel the Welsh or merely to mark the boundary. Mrs Lewis
took an ambivalent attitude to Offa's power: this was the road to
civilisation, sure enough, but its cost was a loss of diversity, of the
quiet kind of flourishing that goes on where things are not being
built and goals driven towards. She herself relished the early Saxon
world, in which concepts of power had not yet been reconfigured;
for in a way the Dark Ages were themselves a version of 'the new reality', were the broken pieces of the biggest plate of all, the Roman
Empire. Some called it darkness, the aftermath of that megaloma-
niacal all-conquering unity, but not Mrs Lewis. She liked it, liked
the untenanted wastes, liked the monasteries where creativity was
quietly nurtured, liked the mystics and the visionaries, the early
religious writings, liked the women who accrued stature in those
formless inchoate centuries, liked the grassroots – the personal –
level on which issues of justice and belief had now to be resolved, in
the absence of that great administrator civilisation.

The point was that this darkness – call it what you will – this
darkness and disorganisation were not mere negation, mere absence.
They were both aftermath and prelude. The etymology of the word
'aftermath' is 'second mowing', a second crop of grass that is sown

and reaped after the harvest is in. Civilisation, order, meaning, belief: these were not sunlit peaks to be reached by a steady climb. They were built and then they fell, were built and fell again or were destroyed. The darkness, the disorganisation that succeeded them had their own existence, their own integrity; were betrothed to civilisation, as sleep is betrothed to activity. In the life of compartments lies the possibility of unity, just as unity contains the prospect of atomisation. Better, in Mrs Lewis's view, to live the compartmentalised, the disorganised life and feel the dark stirrings of creativity, than to dwell in civilised unity, racked by the impulse to destroy.

•

In the mornings I take my daughters to school and at mid-afternoon I pick them up again. I tidy their rooms and do laundry and cook. We spend the evenings mostly alone; I do their homework with them and feed them and put them to bed. Every few days they go to their father's and then the house is empty. At first these interludes were difficult to bear. Now they have a kind of neutrality about them, something firm but blank, something faintly accusatory despite the blankness. It is as though these solitary hours, in which for the first time in many years nothing is expected or required of me, are my spoils of war, are what I have received in exchange for all this conflict. I live them one after another. I swallow them down like hospital food. In this way I am kept alive.

Call yourself a feminist, my husband would say to me, disgustedly, in the raw bitter weeks after we separated. He believed he had taken the part of woman in our marriage, and seemed to expect

me to defend him against myself, the male oppressor. He felt it was
womanly to shop and cook, to collect the children from school. Yet
it was when I myself did those things that I often felt most unsexed.
My own mother had not seemed beautiful to me in the exercise of
her maternal duties: likewise they seemed to threaten, not enhance,
her womanliness. In those days we lived in a village in the flat
Suffolk countryside; she seemed to spend a great deal of time on
the telephone. The sound of her voice talking as though to itself
was mesmerising. To me her phrases sounded scripted, her laughter
slightly artificial. I suspected her of using a special voice, like an
actress. Who was she, this woman on the telephone? My mother
was someone I knew only from the inside; I shared her point of
view, seemed to dwell within her boredom or pleasure or irritation.
Her persona was where I lived, unseeing. How could I know what
my mother was? How could I see her? For her attention felt like the
glance of some inner eye that never looked at me straight, that took
its knowledge from my own private knowledge of myself.

It was only when she was with other people that, as a child,
I was able to notice her objectively. Sometimes she would have a
female friend round to lunch and then all at once there it would
be, my mother's face. Suddenly I could see her, could compare her
to this other woman and find her better or worse, could see her being liked or envied or provoked, could know her particular habits
and her atmosphere, which were not those of this other. At such
times her persona, my dwelling-place, was inaccessible to me, darkened, like an empty house. If I knocked at the door I was curtly —
sometimes roughly — despatched. Her body, usually so extensive, so
carelessly ubiquitous, seemed to have been packed up and put away.
And she too was locked out, relieved for a while of the business of

being herself. Instead she was performing; she was pure story, told badly or well.

Her friends were generally mothers too, women whose geography I recognised, the sense of an enigma that lay all around their masks of make-up and talk like open countryside around a city. You could never get out into that countryside but you knew it was there. She did have one friend, Sally, who was different from the others. At the time I didn't understand why, but now I do: Sally didn't have children. She was a large woman, a wit, though her face was sad. You could walk around in the sadness of her mouth and eyes; it was open to everyone. She came once when my mother had made a chocolate cake, for which she tried to give Sally the recipe. Sally said, 'If I made that cake I'd just eat the whole thing in one sitting.' I had never heard of a woman eating a whole cake. It struck me as a tremendous feat, like weightlifting. But I could tell that my mother didn't like this remark. In some obscure sense Sally had given the game away. Not knowing any better, she had opened up a chink in the tall wall of womanhood, and given me a rare glimpse of what was on the other side.

•

Of certain parts of life there can be no foreknowledge – war, for instance. The soldier going to war for the first time does not know how he will behave when confronted by an armed enemy. He does not know this part of himself. Is he killer or coward? When confronted he will respond, yet he doesn't know in advance what his response will be.

My husband said that he wanted half of everything, including the children. No, I said. What do you mean no, he said. This was on the telephone. I looked out of the window at the garden, a rectangle among other urban rectangles, the boundaries prowled by cats. Lately our garden had become overgrown. The beds were drowning in weeds. The grass was long, like hair. But no matter how disorderly it became the grid would be undisturbed: the other rectangles would hold their shape regardless.

You can't divide people in half, I said.

They should be with me half the time, he said.

They're my children, I said. They belong to me.

In Greek drama, to traduce biological human roles is to court the change that is death, the death that is change. The vengeful mother, the selfish father, the perverted family, the murderous child – these are the bloody roads to democracy, to justice. The children belong to me: once I would have criticised such a sentiment severely, but of certain parts of life there can be no foreknowledge. Where had this heresy gestated? If it was part of me, where had it lived for all those years, in our egalitarian household? Where had it hidden itself? My mother liked to talk about the early English Catholics forced to live and worship in secrecy, sleeping in cupboards or underneath the floorboards. To her it seemed extraordinary that the true beliefs should have to hide themselves. Was this, in fact, a persecuted truth, and our own way of life the heresy?

I said it again: I couldn't help myself. I said it to my friend Eleanor, that the children belonged to me. Eleanor has a job, is often away for weeks at a time; her husband takes over when she's not there, putting their children to bed, handing them over to the nanny in the morning. Eleanor pursed her mouth and disapprovingly shook her head a little. Children belong just as much to their

fathers as their mothers, she said. I said to my friend Anna, who
has no job and four children, the children belong to me. Anna's
husband works long hours. She manages the children largely alone,
as I now do. Yes, she said, they're your children. You're the one they
need. They should be your number one priority.

It has existed in a kind of banishment, my flesh history with
my daughters. Have I been, as a mother, denied? The long pilgrim-
age of pregnancy with its wonders and abasements, the apotheosis
of childbirth, the sacking and slow rebuilding of every last corner of
my private world that motherhood has entailed – all unmentioned,
willfully or casually forgotten as time has passed, the dark ages on
which I now feel the civilisation of our family has been built. And
I was part of that pact of silence, in a way: it was a condition of the
treaty that gave me my equality, that I would not invoke the primi-
tivism of the mother, her innate superiority, that voodoo in the
face of which the mechanism of equal rights breaks down. My own
mother once wept at the supper table, wildly accusing us of never
having thanked her for giving birth to us. And we joked about it
later, cruel teenaged sophisticates. We felt uneasy, and rightly so:
we had been unjustly blamed. Wasn't it my father who should have
thanked her, for giving form and substance, continuance, to himself? Instead his own contribution, his work, ran parallel to hers:
it was she who had to be grateful to him, superficially at least. For
years he had gone to the office and come back again, regular as a
Swiss train, as authorised as she was illicit. The rationality of this
behaviour was what irrationalised hers, for her womanhood was all
imposition and cause, all profligacy, was a kind of problem to which
his work was the solution. How could she expect gratitude for what
no one seemed to think of as a gift? Through her we all of us served

the cause of life: she was the exacting representative of our dumb master, nature. She gave, as nature gives, but we were not going to survive in nature on mere gratitude. We had to tame, to cultivate her gifts; and increasingly, we ourselves took all the credit for the results. We were in league with civilisation.

Like God, my father expressed himself through absence: it was easier, perhaps, to be grateful to someone who wasn't there. He too seemed to obey the call of civilisation, to recognise it when it spoke. As rational beings we allied ourselves with him, against the paganism of my mother, her cycles of emotion, her gaze forever dwelling on what was done and past or on the relieving blankness of what was yet to come. These qualities seemed to be without origin: they belonged neither to motherhood nor to herself, but to some eternal fact that arose out of the conjunction of the two. I knew, of course, that once upon a time she had had her own reality, had lived as it were in real time. In the wedding photograph that stood on the mantelpiece, her slenderness was always arresting. There she stood in white, the sacrificial victim: a narrow-waisted smiling beauty, as compact as a seed. The key, the genius of it all, seemed to lie in how little of her there was. In the finely graven lines of her beauty our whole sprawling future was encrypted. That youthful beauty was gone now, all used up, like the oil that is sucked out of the earth for the purpose of combustion. The world has grown hectic, disorganised, wasteful on oil. Sometimes, looking at that photograph, my family seemed like the bloated product of my mother's beauty.

But for me the notion of a woman's beauty had somewhere in the course of things become theoretical, like the immigrant's notion of home. And in the generational transition between my mother and myself a migration of sorts had indeed occurred. My mother may have been my place of birth, but my adopted nationality was my father's. She had aspired to marriage and motherhood, to being desired and possessed by a man in a way that would legitimise her. I myself was the fruit of those aspirations, but somehow, in the evolution from her to me, it had become my business to legitimise myself. Yet my father's aspirations – to succeed, to win, to provide – did not quite fit me either: they were like a suit of clothes made for someone else, but they were what was available. So I wore them and felt a little uncomfortable, a little unsexed, but clothed all the same. Cross-dressed I met with approval, for a good school report, a high grade. I got into Oxford, my sister to Cambridge, immigrants to the new country of sexual equality achieving assimilation through the second generation.

One is formed by what one's parents say and do; and one is formed by what one's parents are. But what happens when what they say and what they are don't match? My father, a man, advanced male values to us, his daughters. And my mother, a woman, did the same. So it was my mother who didn't match, who didn't make sense. We belong as much to our moment in history as to our parents: I suppose it would have been reprehensible, in Britain in the late twentieth century, for her to have told us not to worry about our maths, that the important thing was to find a nice husband to support us. Yet her own mother had probably told her precisely that. There was nothing, as a woman, she could bequeath us; nothing to pass on from mother to daughter but these adulterated male values. And of that forsaken homeland, beauty, which now lay so despoiled – as the countryside around our Suffolk home was in the years of my growing up despoiled, disfigured by new roads and houses that it pained my oversensitive eyes to look at – of beauty, a woman's beauty, of the place I had come from I knew nothing at all. I didn't know its manners or its customs. I didn't speak its language. In that world of femininity where I had the right to claim citizenship, I was an alien.

•

Call yourself a feminist, my husband says. And perhaps one of these days I'll say to him, yes, you're right. I shouldn't call myself a feminist. You're right. I'm so terribly sorry.

And in a way, I'll mean it. What is a feminist, anyway? What does it mean, to call yourself one? There are men who call themselves feminists. There are women who are anti-feminist. A feminist man is a bit like a vegetarian: it's the humanitarian principle he's defending, I suppose. Sometimes feminism seems to involve so much criticism of female modes of being that you could be forgiven for thinking that a feminist is a woman who hates women, hates them for being such saps. Then again, the feminist is supposed to hate men. She is said to scorn the physical and emotional servitude they exact. Apparently she calls them *the enemy*.

In any case, she wouldn't be found haunting the scene of the crime, as it were; loitering in the kitchen, in the maternity ward, at the school gate. She knows that her womanhood is a fraud, manufactured by others for their own convenience; she knows that women are not born but made. So she stays away from it, the kitchen, the maternity ward, like the alcoholic stays away from the bottle. Some alcoholics have a fantasy of modest social drinking: they just haven't been through enough cycles of failure yet. The woman who thinks she can choose femininity, can toy with it like the social drinker toys with wine – well she's asking for it, asking to be undone, devoured, asking to spend her life perpetrating a new fraud, manufacturing a new fake identity, only this time it's her equality that's fake. Either she's doing twice as much as she did before, or she sacrifices her equality and does less than she should. She's two women, or she's half a woman. And either way she'll have to say, because she chose it, that she's enjoying herself.

So I suppose a feminist shouldn't get married. She shouldn't have a joint bank account or a house in joint names. Perhaps she shouldn't have children either, girl children whose surname is not their mother's but their father's, so that when she travels abroad with them they have to swear to the man at passport control that she *is* their mother. No, I shouldn't have called myself a feminist, because what I said didn't match with what I was: just like my mother, only the other way around.

What I lived as feminism were in fact the male values my parents, among others, well-meaningly bequeathed me – the cross-dressing values of my father, and the anti-feminine values of my mother. So I am not a feminist. I am a self-hating transvestite.

•

Like many women I know, I have never been supported financially by a man. This is anecdotal information – women have a weakness for that. And perhaps a feminist is someone who possesses this personalising trait to a larger than average degree: she is an autobiographer, an artist of the self. She acts as an interface between private and public, just as women always have, except that the feminist does it in reverse. She does not propitiate: she objects. She's a woman turned inside out.

If you live long enough, the anecdotal becomes the statistical in any case. You emerge with your cohorts out of the jungle of middle life, each possessing your own private knowledge of courage or cowardice, and do a quick head-count, an inventory of missing limbs. I know women with four children and women with no children, divorced women and married women, successful and compromised women, apologetic, ambitious and contented women, women who are unfulfilled or accepting, selfless and frustrated women. And some of them, it is true, are not financially dependent on men. What can I say about the ones that are? That they're usually full-time mothers. And that they live more through their children. That's how it seems to me. The child goes through the full-time mother like a dye through water: there is no part of her that remains uncoloured. The child's triumphs and losses are her triumphs and losses. The child's beauty is her beauty, as is the child's unacceptability. And because management of the child is her job, her own management of the world is conducted through it. Her subjectivity has more than one source, and only a single outlet. This can result in extreme competence: some of my friends claim to find such women frightening or threatening. These friends are generally women who sustain more than one identity out of a single self, and hence perhaps fear accusations of extreme incompetence. Their power is diffuse: they never feel it collected in one place, and as a result they don't know how much of it there is, whether they have less or more power than that curiously titled creature, the stay-at-home mum, or indeed than their male colleagues at work who must, I suppose, share at least some of their feelings of scatteration.

A few of these working-mother friends of mine have taken the occasional domestic furlough, usually in the early years of parenthood. Like wanted criminals finally run to ground, they surrender with their hands up: yes, it was all too much, too unworkable, the running hither and thither, the guilt, the pressure at work, the pressure at home, the question of why – if you were never going to see them – you went to the trouble of having children in the first place. So they decide to stay at home for a year or two and even things up a bit, like the cake mixture the recipe tells you to divide between two tins, of which there always seems to be more in one than the other. Their husbands also work, live in the same houses and parent the same children, yet don't seem to experience quite the same measure of conflict. In fact, sometimes they actually look like they're better at being working parents than women are – insufferable male superiority!

But a man commits no particular heresy against his sex by being a good father, and working is part of what a good father does. The working mother, on the other hand, is traducing her role in the founding myths of civilisation on a daily basis – no wonder she's a little harassed. She's trying to defy her own deep-seated relationship with gravity. I read somewhere that a space station is always slowly falling back to earth, and that every few months or so a rocket has to be sent to push it back out again. In rather the same way, a woman is forever dragged at by an imperceptible force of biological conformism; her life is relentlessly iterative; it requires energy to keep her in orbit. Year after year she'll do it, but if one year the rocket doesn't come then down she'll go.

The stay-at-home mum often describes herself as lucky: that's her pitch, her line, should anyone – a working mother, for instance – care to enquire. We're so lucky that James's salary means I don't have to work, she'll say, as though she took a huge punt on a single

horse and found that she'd backed a winner. You don't catch a man
saying he feels lucky to be able to go to the office every day. Yet the
stay-at-home mum often calls it a privilege, to be 'allowed' to do her
traditional and entirely unexceptional domestic work. It's a defen-
sive statement, of course – she doesn't want to be thought of as lazy
or unambitious – and like much defensiveness it (barely) conceals a
core of aggression. Yet presumably she is elated when her daughter
comes top in the maths test, gets a place at Cambridge, becomes a
nuclear physicist. Does she wish it for her daughter, that privilege,
the time-immemorial life at home with children? Or does she think
this is a riddle that someone in the future will somehow just solve,
like scientists inventing the cure for cancer?

I remember, when my own children were born, when I first
held them and fed them and talked to them, feeling a great awareness of this new, foreign aspect of myself that was in me and yet
did not seem to be of me. It was as though I had suddenly acquired
the ability to speak Russian: what I could do – this women's work –
had so much form of its own, yet I didn't know where my knowledge of it had come from. In some ways I wanted to claim the
knowledge as mine, as innate, but to do that seemed to involve a
strange kind of dishonesty, a pretending. But how could I pretend
to be what I already was? I felt inhabited by a second self, a twin
whose jest it was – in the way of twins – to appear to be me while
doing things that were alien to my own character. Yet this twin
was not apparently malign: she was just asking for a degree of freedom, a temporary release from the strict protocol of identity. She
wanted to act as a woman, a generic woman, but character is not
generic. It is entirely and utterly specific. To act as a mother, I had
to suspend my own character, which had evolved on a diet of male

values. And my habitat, my environment, had evolved that way too.
An adaptation would be required. But who was going to do the
adapting? I was aware, in those early days, that my behaviour was
strange to the people who knew me well. It was as though I had
been brainwashed, taken over by a cult religion. I had gone away –
I couldn't be reached on the usual number. And yet this cult,
motherhood, was not a place where I could actually live. It reflected
nothing about me: its literature and practices, its values, its codes
of conduct, its aesthetic were not mine. It was generic too: like any
cult, it demanded a complete surrender of identity to belong to it.
So for a while I didn't belong anywhere. As the mother of young
children I was homeless, drifting, itinerant. And I felt an inadmis-
sible pity for myself and for my daughters in those years. It seemed,
almost, catastrophic to me, the disenchantment of this contact with
womanhood. Like the adopted child who finally locates its parents
only to discover that they are loveless strangers, my inability to
find a home as a mother impressed me as something not about the
world but about my own unwantedness. I seemed, as a woman, to
be extraneous.

And so I did two things: I reverted to my old male-inflected
identity; and I conscripted my husband into care of the children.
He was to take the part of that twin, femininity. He was to offer
her a body of her own to shelter in, for she didn't seem able to find
peace in me. My notion was that we would live together as two
hybrids, each of us half male and half female. That was equality,
was it not? He gave up his law job, and I gave up the exclusivity
of my primitive maternal right over the children. These were our
preparatory sacrifices to the new gods, whose future protection we
hoped to live under. Ten years later, sitting in a solicitor's office on a

noisy main road in north London, my maternalism did indeed seem primitive to me, almost barbaric. The children belong to me – this was not the kind of rudimentary phrase-making I generally went in for. Yet it was the only thought in my head, there in the chrome and glass office, with the petite solicitor in tailored black sitting opposite. I was thin and gaunt with distress, yet in her presence I felt enormous, rough-hewn, a maternal rock encrusted with ancient ugly emotion. She told me I had no rights of any kind. The law in these cases didn't operate on the basis of rights. What mattered was the precedent, and the precedent could be as unprecedented as you liked. So there was no primitive reality after all, it seemed. There was no such thing as a mother, a father. There was only civilisation. She told me I was obliged to support my husband financially, possibly forever. But he's a qualified lawyer, I said. And I'm just a writer. What I meant was, he's a man. And I'm just a woman. The old voodoo still banging its drum, there in the heart of marital darkness. The solicitor raised her slender eyebrows, gave me a bitter little smile. Well, then he knew exactly what he was doing, she said.

•

Summer came, clanging days of glaring sunshine in the seaside town where I live, the gulls screaming in the early dawn, a glittering agitation everywhere, the water a vista of smashed light. I could no longer sleep; my consciousness filled up with the lumber of dreams, of broken-edged sections of the past heaving and stirring in the undertow. At the school gate, collecting my daughters, the other women looked somehow quaint to me, as people look when seen across a distance. I saw them as though from the annihilated emptiness of the ocean, people inhabiting land, inhabiting a construction. They had not destroyed their homes. Why had I destroyed my home? Visiting my sister, I sat in her kitchen while she folded laundry. I watched her fold her husband's shirts, his trousers. It shocked me to see these male garments, to see her touching them. She seemed to be touching something forbidden. Her right to handle these forbidden items overwhelmed me.

You know the law, my husband said over the phone. He was referring to my obligation to give him money.

I know what's right, I said.

Call yourself a feminist, he said.

What I need is a wife, jokes the stressed-out feminist career woman, and everyone laughs. The joke is that the feminist's pursuit of male values has led her to the threshold of female exploitation. This is irony. Get it? The feminist scorns that silly complicit creature the housewife. Her first feminist act may have been to try to liberate her own housewife mother, only to discover that rescue was neither wanted nor required. I hated my mother's unwaged status, her servitude, her domesticity, undoubtedly more than she herself did, for she never said she disliked them at all. Yet I stood accused of recreating exactly those conditions in my own adult life. I had hated my husband's unwaged domesticity just as much as I had hated my mother's; and he, like her, had claimed to be contented with his lot. Why had I hated it so? Because it represented dependence. But there was more to it than that, for it might be said that dependence is an agreement between two people. My father depended on my mother too: he couldn't cook a meal, or look after children from the office. They were two halves that made up a whole. What, morally speaking, is half a person? Yet the two

halves were not the same: in a sense my parents were a single compartmentalised human being. My father's half was very different
from my mother's, but despite the difference neither half made any
sense on its own. So it was in the difference that the problem lay.

My notion of half was more like the earthworm's: you cut it in
two, but each half remains an earthworm, wriggling and fending
for itself. I earned the money in our household, did my share of the
cooking and cleaning, paid someone to look after the children while
I worked, picked them up from school once they were older. And
my husband helped. It was his phrase, and still is: he helped me. I
was the compartmentalised modern woman, the woman having it
all, and he helped me to be it, to have it. But I didn't want help: I
wanted equality. In fact, this idea of help began to annoy me. Why
couldn't we be the same? Why couldn't he be compartmentalised
too? And why, exactly, was it helpful for a man to look after his own
children, or cook the food that he himself would eat? Helpful is
what a good child is to its mother. A helpful person is someone who
performs duties outside their own sphere of responsibility, out of the
kindness of their heart. Help is dangerous because it exists outside
the human economy: the only payment for help is gratitude. And
did I not have something of the same gratuitous tone where my
wage-earning was concerned? Did I not think there was something
awfully helpful about me, a woman, supporting my own family?

And so I felt, beneath the reconfigured surface of things, the
tension of the old orthodoxies. We were a man and a woman who
in our struggle for equality had simply changed clothes. We were
two transvestites, a transvestite couple – well, why not? Except that
I did both things, was both man and woman, while my husband –
meaning well – only did one. Once, a female friend confessed to

me that she admired our life but couldn't have lived it herself. She admitted the reason – that she would no longer respect her husband if he became a wife. The admiration interested me. What, precisely, was being admired? And how could what was admirable entail the loss of respect?

Sometimes my awareness of my own competence alarmed me. How would I remain attached to the world if not by need? I didn't appear to need anyone: I could do it all myself. I could do everything. I was both halves: did that mean I was whole? In a sense I was living at the high point of feminist possibility: there was no blueprint beyond 'having it all'. The richness of that phrase, its suggestion of an unabashed splendour, was apposite. To have both motherhood and work was to have two lives instead of one, was a stunning refinement of historical female experience, and to the people who complained that having it all meant doing it all I would have said, yes, of course it does. You don't get 'all' for nothing. 'Having it all', like any form of success, requires hard work. It requires an adoption of the heroic mode of being. But the hero is solitary, forever searching out the holy grail, her belief that she is exceptional perhaps only a disguise for the fact that she is essentially alone.

So I was both man and woman, but over time the woman sickened, for her gratifications were fewer. I had to keep out of the way, keep out of the kitchen, keep a certain distance from my children, not only to define my husband's femininity but to appease my own male values. The oldest trick in the sexist book is the female need for control of children. I perceived in the sentimentality and narcissism of motherhood a threat to the objectivity that as a writer I valued so highly. But it wasn't control of the children I was necessarily sickening for. It was something subtler – prestige, the prestige that is the mother's reward for the work of bearing her offspring. And that prestige was my husband's. I had given it to him or he had taken it – either way, it was what he got out of our arrangement. And the domestic work I did was in a sense at the service of that prestige, for it encompassed the menial, the trivial, the frankly boring, as though I was busily working behind the scenes to ensure the smooth running of the spectacle on stage. I wasn't male after all – men didn't do drudgery. And I wasn't female either: I felt ugly, for the things that were mine – dirty laundry, VAT returns – were not pretty at all. In fact, there was nothing pretty that gave me back a reflection of myself. I went to Paris for two days with my husband, determined while I was there to have my unkempt hair cut in a French salon. Wasn't this what women did? I wanted to be womanised; I wanted someone to restore to me my lost femininity. A male hairdresser cut off all my hair, giggling as he did it, amusing himself during a boring afternoon at the salon by giving a tired blank-faced mother of two something punky and *nouvelle vague*. Afterwards I wandered in the Paris streets, anxiously catching my reflection in shop windows. Had a transformation occurred, or a defacement? I wasn't sure. My husband wasn't sure either. It seemed terrible that between us we couldn't establish the truth. It seemed terrible, in broad daylight, in those public anonymous streets, not to know.

•

Sometimes, in the bath, the children cry. Their nakedness, or the warm water, or the comfort of the old routine – something, anyway, dislodges their sticking-plaster emotions and shows the wound beneath. It is my belief that I gave them that wound, so now I must take all the blame. Another version of the heroic, where the hero and the villain are hard to tell apart.

I wounded them and in this way I learned truly to love them. Or rather, I admitted it, admitted this love, admitted how much of it there was. I externalised it: internalised, it had been an instrument of self-torture. But now it was out in the world, visible, practical. What is a loving mother? It is someone whose self-interest has been displaced into her actual children. Her children's suffering causes her more pain than her own: it is Mary at the foot of the cross. In church, at the Easter service, I used to be struck by the description of Mary's emotional state, for amid that drama of physical torment it was said that she felt as though a sword had been run through her heart. It interested me that such an image was applied to her feelings, an image that came to her from the cold hard outer world, from the physical plane of men. Somehow, in the transition from other to mother, the active becomes passive, the actual theoretical, the physical emotional, the objective subjective. The blow is softened: when my children cry a sword is run through my heart. Yet it is I who am also the cause of their crying. And for a while I am undone by this contradiction, by the difficulty of connecting the person who acted out of self-interest with the heartbroken mother who has succeeded her. It seems to be the fatal and final evolution of the compartmentalised woman, a kind of personality disorder, like schizophrenia.

Winter comes: the days are brief and pale, the sea retracted as though into unconsciousness. The coldly silvered water turns quietly on the shingle. There are long nights of stars and frost, and in the morning frozen puddles lie like little smashed mirrors in the road. We sleep many hours, like people recovering from an operation. Pain is so vivid, yet the stupor of recovery is such that pain's departure often goes unnoticed. You simply realise, one day, that it has gone, leaving a curious blank in the memory, a feeling of transitive mystery, as though the person who suffered is not – not quite – the same as the person who now walks around well. Another compartment has been created, this one for keeping odds and ends in, stray parts of experience, questions for which the answers were never found.

We rearrange the furniture to cover up the gaps. We economise, take in a lodger, get a fishtank. The fish twirl and pirouette eternally amid the fronds, regardless of what day it is. The children go to their father's and come back again. They no longer cry: they complain heartily about the inconvenience of the new arrangements. They have colour in their faces. A friend comes to stay and remarks on the sound of laughter in the house, like birdsong after the silence of winter. But it is winter still: we go to a Christmas carol service and I watch the other families. I watch mother and father and children. And I see it so clearly, as though I were looking in at them through a brightly lit window from the darkness outside; see the story in which they play their roles, their parts, with the whole world as a backdrop. We're not part of that story any more, my children and I. We belong more to the world, in all its risky disorder, its fragmentation, its freedom. The world is constantly evolving, while the family endeavours to stay the same. Updated, refurbished, modernised, but essentially the same. A house in the landscape, both shelter and prison.

We sing the carols, a band of three. I have sung these songs since my earliest recollection, sung them year after year: first as a tradition-loving child in the six-strong conventional family pew; later as a young woman who most ardently called herself a feminist; later still as a wife and mother in whose life these unreconcilable principles – the traditional and the radical, the story and the truth – had out of their hostility hatched a kind of cancer. Looking at the other families I feel our stigma, our loss of prestige: we are like a gypsy caravan parked up among the houses, itinerant, temporary. I see that we have lost a degree of protection, of certainty. I see that I have exchanged one kind of prestige for another, one set of values for another, one scale for another. I see too that we are more open, more capable of receiving than we were; that should the world prove to be a generous and wondrous place, we will perceive its wonders.

I begin to notice, looking in through those imaginary brightly lit windows, that the people inside are looking out. I see the women, these wives and mothers, looking out. They seem happy enough, contented enough, capable enough: they are well dressed, attractive, standing with their men and their children. Yet they look around, their mouths moving. It is as though they are missing something or wondering about something. I remember it so well, what it was to be one of them. Sometimes one of these glances will pass over me and our eyes will briefly meet. And I realise she can't see me, this woman whose eyes have locked with mine. It isn't that she doesn't want to, or is trying not to. It's just that inside it's so bright and outside it's so dark, and so she can't see out, can't see anything at all.

EXTRACTION

The day my husband moved his possessions out of our house I had toothache. It was raining, and all morning the door to the street stood open. The wet air gusted in and the dim hall lay like an opened tomb in the grey daylight. I stood at the bottom of the stairs, my hands over my mouth, like a mime artist pantomiming dismay.

The dentist recommended extraction: the X-ray photograph showed that the tooth was beyond repair. Theoretically, he said, it ought to be possible, but the idiosyncracies of the case were what counted here. The crooked shape of the root made it inaccessible to the long, fine instruments that would kill the nerves. They, the instruments, could not turn corners. And the root, as the X-ray showed, had grown at a right angle to itself halfway down.

Why had it assumed that shape? It was difficult to know, the dentist said. It may have been bent by the pressure of other forces, but there appeared to be an aspect of fate to it too, the response of its own nature to the available conditions. To an extent it had simply chosen to go in that direction. One could not entirely blame the positioning of the other teeth, the spatial properties of the jaw, the condition of the gums; no, the tooth itself would have to an-

swer for its doomed character. It had been in some ineluctable sense
wayward, and now it had put itself beyond reach. A straighter root,
however diseased, could have been redeemed. Superficially the condition of this one was not so bad, but form is destiny; form, not
content, that which is shaped and therefore shapes its own fate.

While the X-ray was taken the dentist and the nurses stepped
back, as one, reflexively turning away and crossing their arms over
their chests. Their soft-shod feet were noiseless as they withdrew in
this synchronised gesture of self-protection: in their white overalls
they stood like acolytes at the ceremony of blood. The dentist, a tall
and broad-shouldered Greek, wore beneath his overall a richly patterned floor-length robe. The wan nurses were silent as they moved
dimly among the white and chrome cabinets at the back of the room,
forever recessed, like figures in the background of a painting. Was
the pain more or less constant, he asked, or were there still phases of
normality in which one could do and think of other things? Had we
reached the point of crisis where our only experience was the experience of suffering, where our only need, our only desire was the desire
to end it? It is terrible to desire the end of something, the absence of
something: desire should belong to life, to presence and not absence.
One should be careful not to live in this inverted state too long; nor,
he said, should one pull out a tooth unless it is absolutely necessary.
Had we, then, reached the moment at which extraction had become
impossible to defer any longer?

It could be said, yes, that the pain no longer had any intermis-
sions. It used to be possible to escape from it at night, in sleep, but
lately it had found out that hiding place too and had broken it
down, like an invader breaking down the door of an ill-defended
fortress. The ease with which the door came down was a crisis in

itself: how fragile, how insubstantial normality was proved to be once pain came to disturb it! Pain is strong and huge and relentless, and 'normality' – that was the word he used, wasn't it? – normality is the fine balance life achieves in the absence of disruption, is the blank register of events and their aftermath, slowly re-stitching and repairing itself, as the surface of a pool gradually becalms itself after a pebble has been thrown in. Normality is capable of resisting nothing and can outlive almost anything. Pain, on the other hand, can destroy whatever it has a mind to. Pain is the bomb that falls, and normality the grass that grows, at length, over the crater. To resist pain one must be as strong as pain, must make of oneself a kind of human bomb-shelter.

The extraction will leave a sizable declivity – a crater of sorts – behind it. It is a molar, centrally placed on the lower right jaw: a large tooth of great practical and personal significance whose disappearance nonetheless will be surprisingly unnoticeable from outside. It will not, of course, grow back. The intimate world of the mouth will suffer irreversible loss. In time, if sufficient resources and effort of will can be found, a simulacrum may be fitted; until then, the other teeth will have to do the work of compensating for the absence. Different modes of eating and chewing might evolve to remove strain from the area; curiously enough, the mirroring molar on the left-hand side is also missing. This is not, then, the first such experience of loss. A major tooth has already decayed and been extracted from this mouth, a history which obviously makes things harder. The current extraction is a darker business because of it. And the question of blame, always so delicate where it is in the nature of things to break down, is altered by this new piece of evidence. It's beginning to look like carelessness, to paraphrase

Oscar Wilde. For a tooth, properly looked after, ought to be able to last a lifetime.

Outside the dentist's windows is a sky of brilliant blue. Yesterday's rain has been succeeded by an outpouring of confident spring sunshine, as unseasonally hot as the other was preternaturally cold and dark. The dentist's room is balmy and bright; the sun sparkles on the steel instruments. The whole place is somewhat decrepit, the narrow building in its higgledy-piggledy street all crooked angles and canting floors, its partition walls and flimsy ceilings thickly muffled in bumpy off-white paper, its beech-patterned beige vinyl rising and falling thinly over the uneven boards. In the reception area there is a small fishtank with electric-green plastic ferns and a bubbling pirate ship sitting on a gravel bed; there are posters of diseased mouths, of infected gums, of the blackened stumps of rotted teeth. The dentist strides superbly around these improvised spaces in his patterned robe, as cheerful and dignified as his visitors are pensive and cowed. His teeth are strong and white and straight, and perhaps for this reason his smile is irrepressible. It lives on the surface, always reappearing, like something buoyant in water: it can't be sunk. It looks, almost, unnatural. It is hard to know whether it represents good fortune – luck – or diligence and hard work. He appears to be happy, but has he always been like that? His partner in the dental practice has teeth as grey as tombstones in an overcrowded graveyard, and a canny, comprehending face; his overall is shabby and creased. From these appearances it might be deduced that one man has the knowledge of failure and the other does not. But how can one really tell? And is it better to be at the mercy of someone who understands pain or who has managed thus far to avoid it?

The dentist rummages in his tray of instruments; the nurses

draw close. He leans forward, a dark shape against the bright window. The sunlit room is silent and there rises a kind of aural transparency through which a deeper background of sound emerges, intricately embroidered like an ocean bed seen through clear water: the sound of passing cars outside, of dogs barking and the distant keening of gulls, of fragments of conversation from the pavements below and music playing somewhere, of phones ringing, pots and pans clattering in a faraway restaurant kitchen, babies crying, workmen faintly hammering, of footsteps, of people breathing, and beneath it all a kind of pulse, the very heartbeat and hydraulics of the day. The dentist has a pair of pliers in his hand. Their factuality amid this impalpable veil of sound is unmistakable. They are simple and heavy and black. He wields them, drawing closer. He enters the mouth and with the arms of the pliers lays a ferocious metallic grip on the tooth. Every process has been passed through, except this one. First there was the long process of decay itself, brewing day after day in the darkness of the root; then the birth of pain, a seed that grew and branched, seeking out consciousness, awareness, like a plant seeks light and thereby blots it out; then the negotiations, consciousness negotiating with pain, trying to pacify and mollify it, to control and contain it, to dull it and hence live with it; then crisis, decision, action, a date and time decided on at which extraction would occur and the situation be brought to an end. But the contact of steel with human flesh has a reality of its own. It is happening: things are being changed, having been unable to change themselves.

The dentist wrenches and wrenches amid the soft tissues. His intervention seems allied somehow with death, yet it belongs to life, for its purpose is to liberate the sufferer from the cause of suffering.

Its purpose is to separate what will not naturally separate itself. But it is cold and hard, insensate, brutal. It is called violence: people are forever trying to find alternatives to it, but they seldom work.

The dentist speaks.

'More force is required,' he says.

The nurse hands him a chisel. He positions it on the edge of the jaw and places the flat tip between the tooth and the gum. He pushes down, straining so hard that his smile becomes a grimace. Presently he stands to improve his leverage. He uses both hands; he stands on tiptoe, bearing down with shaking arms. The tooth resists and resists, and when at last it gives way it does so too easily, so that the chisel spends its force upwards, hitting the teeth above. They take the blow, these innocent teeth, rocking in their moorings; they loosen, but they stay where they are. The dentist holds up the bloody tooth between his trembling fingers. He is beaming again, though with less intensity. A little consternation threads his brow. Violence is so unwieldy, so difficult to control. There is collateral damage; the fine mesh of life is torn. He has caused unnecessary pain, and trauma to the other teeth. He feels bad about it. He is surprised.

'I didn't expect it to come out like that,' he says. 'I'm sorry.'

'Please don't worry,' I say, with difficulty. 'I'll be all right.'

'I will pack the wound with dressings,' he says. 'You need to change them every two hours. The bleeding should stop by tomorrow but you won't be able to eat normally for a while. Soft things, that's all. And cold will feel more pleasant.' He smiles, happy again. 'Make sure you buy yourself a big ice cream on the way home.'

•

Home: as a child I loved my grandmother's house, a semi-detached Edwardian villa in a Hertfordshire suburb with mullioned windows on whose sills china shepherdesses stood, and King Charles spaniels with enamelled waterfalls of porcelain hair. In the gas-scented kitchen my grandmother served shepherd's pie with frozen peas; I was put to bed in the little room upstairs whose window looked out on the rectangle of front garden with its laid redbrick path and gate, and beneath the faded pink candlewick bedspread and thick stiff sheets succumbed to the force of these sights and smells and textures which, though not human, seemed to define humanness. Touching the ornaments in my grandmother's sitting room, from whose windows could be seen the long, sloping back lawn that led down to the railway line, I felt visible; the smell of the room where she and my grandfather slept in their mahogany bed, of the cold narrow lavatory, of the small pantry where the constituents of her plain English cooking dwelled, were so distinct that they made me distinct too, just as in the garden the dark foliage of the perennial shrubs made it possible to see the filigree spiders' webs spun across their empty spaces. My mother grew up in that house: her amniotic atmosphere was there too in the potent rooms, as it was in my own consciousness, ineradicable.

As an adolescent I went to stay once with my grandmother alone; I ate in the linoleum-floored kitchen, sat amongst the ornaments in the sitting room, slept under the candlewick bedspread in the little room that seemed somewhat shrunken now, solidified, its reality and my own no longer intertwined. I could not, try as I might, feel like the child I once was. During those hours the whole merging of human and non-human came unravelled, for it became clear to me that the human history these rooms embodied could never be retrieved and released back into the world. A few years later the house was sold: other people live there now. In the compact little cottage to which my grandmother moved, a handful of the familiar objects are still exhibited, a trace of the familiar smell still remains; like a footprint in the sand after the tide has washed over it, her impression is being gradually erased.

In a box in an upstairs room of my house lie the deeds of the building, dating its successive transfers in ownership back to its construction in 1832. A sea captain had first bought the land from a farmer, one of several parcels of green hillside running down to the sea which together would form the basis of a sloping Regency terrace. The land is specified as having been pasture for grazing cattle: at the bottom of the hill the shingle beach shelves into the water, a straight and simple coastline at which the large ocean often seems to wait, as though lacking a means of intercourse with the land that bounds it. Fifty or sixty miles along, in Dorset, the relationship between the two is more dramatic, and dramatised, the limestone sculpted into extraordinary shapes by the pressing, insistent water, which is forever harassing and caressing its rocky mate, half predator and half lover. The resistant rock bears the marks of these attentions, either acquiescent or violated, it's hard to tell. Its beauty and its deformity are its destiny, an interface lacking from the flat shoreline here, with its placidly frigid geology. Here the broad blank sea has no choice but to become reflective, as though it is not living but dreaming; sometimes utterly still, a shimmering unconscious shield of light, at others upset, blindly thrashing and roiling, unable to vent itself on anything tangible and real. There is nothing here for it to destroy, to affect: in the morning, after a storm, the beach will sometimes be littered with a great quantity of something particular, as though this is what has plagued its unconscious – hundreds of dead starfish, for instance, and once, mile after mile of sawn pine planks. These occasional expectorations, so unnatural and strange, seem to signify a certain malaise, a sickness that I interpret as frustration. I imagine the cattle grazing here once, slumbrous too, beside the comatose sea; imagine the land swept by unimpeded waves of shadow and light, by great gauzy veils of rain, by winds roaming unconstricted over the openness, and by darkness, by dark nights of wind and rain, the sea tossing and fretful, the rain hurling itself out of the sky, the wind raving up the bare hill and away among the black shapes of the Downs, and nowhere to shelter, no front door to close against the night.

In the big upstairs room whose windows go all the way down to the floor there are two enormous, ornate gilt hooks mysteriously screwed into the high ceiling. One day, coming out of the house, I met an old woman standing outside on the pavement looking up at these windows. She told me that when she was younger she lived in this road and often used to stand where she was now, listening to the sound of singing that came out of them. It was the lady who owned the house then who was singing: she was an opera singer, and she lived here with a man who played a stringed instrument, a lute or perhaps a guitar, or maybe it was a mandolin. She it was who put the hooks into the ceiling: she hung her hammock from them and would sit at one end, singing, with her man at the other accompanying her, both of them swinging in the breezes from the open windows. At the time this image pierced me with a feeling that was almost pain, for that room was my bedroom and I often lay and looked at those hooks, seeing something in the enigma of them to which I could never give an exact name; in their golden extrava-

gance and lack of usefulness they tantalised me and reproached
me at the same time, for though I didn't know what they were for
I knew some force had put them there whose nature I both recognised and denied. These mysterious objects, these ferocious opulent
hooks, expressed its terror and its beauty; they were, I felt sure, the
opposite of a gutless adornment. Other people, seeing them, would
sometimes betray something of my own alarm, as though these
were the golden claws of an angry deity we had forgotten to placate.
And they had fastened on my room, these claws, to remind me of
something I didn't seem to know or couldn't remember, something
to do with happiness, and with the power of the unknown to undo
the known. What are they for? people would ask, gazing at them
quizzically. And I would always answer that I didn't know.

·

There is a more convenient dentist, in fact. Her practice is much
closer to my house. This dentist is glamorous, with blonde waved
hair and a slender, buxom figure like a fifties film star. Sometimes
I see her slim calves disappearing up the grimy stairwell to the
building, hear the rapid tick-tack of her high-heeled shoes. She
wears little tailored outfits in beautiful colours, primrose and ma-
genta, scarlet and pistachio green. She has a slightly distressed look
about her as she comes and goes; an air of apprehension haunts her
rosebud expression, like the film star in the suspenseful phase of the
drama. Will the mystery resolve itself? Will the impossible become
possible? Will our heroine win the day? In the mornings the road is
full of rubbish, of litter the maritime winds blow across the pavements, of broken bottles and discarded food the seagulls tug from

the plastic bags left out for the binmen. The dentist picks her way through it, the collar of her coat turned up, like a tragic starlet in a Paris backstreet.

I went to her practice once, made an appointment and climbed the narrow stairs to the first floor with my daughters. We needed to register with a dentist, and though it looked like we were simply following the promptings of fate in coming here, some secret vanity made me want the exotic dentist for her own sake, for like the golden hooks in my bedroom ceiling she represented my own forsaken sense of glamour, was another manifestation of the deity who found it so provoking to be denied. It was dark up there, and tenebrous, though outside it was a bright afternoon. A single bulb lit the gloomy hall. In the waiting room the blinds were down. I stood with my daughters at the vacant reception desk. We waited five minutes, ten. Presently I spoke to someone passing and was told to keep waiting. I could hear voices in other rooms, and footsteps going rapidly to and fro. I realised that something was happening: there was a feeling of drama here, a dark sense of incident in the muffled voices and the deserted desk. I heard the sound of drilling, and then more voices, low and urgent.

'Has he come round?' someone said.

'He doesn't want to wake up.' This was the dentist's voice.

'Try again.'

I moved out into the hall and saw through the partly opened door the room the voices were coming from. I could see the dentist's back: she was wearing a red silk blouse today, tightly cinched at the waist with a belt; and, unusually, trousers over her vertiginous heels. Her yellow hair flowed in serpentine waves over her shoulders. She was bending over the dentist's chair, in which lay the unconscious body of a man. Another woman, a nurse I suppose, was there too: through the gap in the door I saw the two women, together, stooped over the man's body. They shook him and prodded him. They called in his ear. He lay there like a broken toy they had, between them, destroyed; as though, fascinated by their power over him, they had forgotten for a moment his fallibility. I went back to the waiting room, where my daughters still stood. Their faces were uncertain. Along the hall the man had begun to groan, loud and long and terrible groans that filled the gloomy half-darkness of the waiting room.

'I think we should go,' I said. 'I think we should come back another time.'

My daughters looked more uncertain still.

'Why?' they said.

Their response surprised me. Could they not see for themselves that things were not right? The man groaned and bellowed down the hall. Was this what a world run by women looked like? A woman, I thought, should be more than a mere impersonator. My daughters' anxious faces, the groaning man, the deserted reception desk in the shadowy waiting room: in the presence of these things I felt the presence of failure. It was I who had brought them here, who had made the appointment; now I was saying we had to go.

'There's been a mix-up,' I said. 'I was sure the appointment was today but they haven't got it written down.'

'Oh,' they said.

'Perhaps we'll find a different dentist,' I said. 'Perhaps this one isn't very well organised.'

They looked a little suspicious – after all, I had made much of the proximity of this dentist to our house. What was going on here?

Out in the shadowy hall, we met the dentist herself, hastening from her room. She looked flushed and harried; she had her coat on with the collar turned up. Behind her the man still lay splayed in the chair, groaning dreadfully. The nurse appeared in another doorway.

'Is he all right?' she said.

'He'll live,' said the dentist harshly. 'He feels a bit sick, that's all. I'm just going to buy him a can of Coke.'

She pushed past us, closing her collar around her throat with a flash of red-painted fingernails. I smelled her perfume, heard the jingle of coins in her pocket. She tick-tacked away down the stairs.

COUPLES

Everywhere people are in couples. On the corner of my road I pass a man and a woman, kissing in the passing traffic. I pass a heavily tattooed couple coming back side by side from the shops, their arms full of purchases, their children in a line behind them like ducklings. I pass a man and a woman with Down's Syndrome, holding hands. They make it seem so easy, to love.

The weather is fine for the time of year. In the mornings the sun streams through the windows into the half-empty rooms, like sun falling on a ruin. The timbers creak with the unaccustomed warmth, sending the sound of footfalls around the house. They travel eerily up and down the stairs and across the ceilings overhead, as though there were someone in the room above who had crossed to the window to look out. The water mutters in the pipes; periodically the boiler ignites, choking and grumbling cholerically in the basement. One day it finally falls silent; the dishwasher breaks, the drains clog, the knobs of doors and cupboards come away unexpectedly in the hand. There is the sound of dripping water, and a dark stain spreads across the kitchen wall, the plaster bulging and flaking like afflicted skin. The children's hamsters scuttle in their separate cages, oblivious. They can't live together, for as a species they are too irascible. They condemn themselves to solitude, immersed in their routines of sleeping and gnawing and burrowing. Sometimes they climb the bars at the sides of the cages and look out with inquisitive bead-bright eyes, as though, having issued from their self-absorption, they now expect something to happen. In a way they are too trusting, for no one notices their changes of circumstance. At night the high-pitched sound of them running on their separate wheels fills the dark silent house.

A man comes to look at the spare room. He is pale and flaxenhaired, with small, almost colourless eyes and sharp little wolverine teeth. He has a tiny battered car he parks in the street outside. Every now and then he goes to the sitting-room window to check for traffic wardens. The room was advertised for rent in the local paper: the phone has rung and rung every day for a week. As soon as I replace the receiver it rings again; I go out and return to find the answering machine full, the red light blinking. Nearly all the calls are from men, men from everywhere and nowhere, men of all kinds: young men and old, foreign and local, gruff and loquacious, determined and indifferent, and all apparently untethered, alone, briefly circling the fixed point of my house while held at some unbreachable distance, like barren planets orbiting a star in the blackness of outer space. Sometimes there is interference on the line, crackling, the sound of windy mountaintops. I am calling about the room. I am calling to enquire about the room. Once or twice a woman has rung: she is looking for somewhere for herself and her boyfriend. She is part of a couple – do I have a problem with that? Her boyfriend works at the bar, the casino, the club down at the marina. Her boyfriend works nights: he likes to sleep during the day. She herself wants to do a course, in aromatherapy, nutrition, languages;

she's thinking about asking at the university; she isn't quite sure. She and her boyfriend are very relaxed. They are very chilled. They like relaxed, chilled people, people with no worries. They don't like to get stressed. Do I have a problem with that? I'm sorry, I say. I live here with my children. It's their home. I'm sorry.

Then one afternoon a man rings sounding anxious and purposeful, as though he's lost something but is certain to find it again at any moment. His voice suggests neither need nor imposition: this is the man who now stands in my house, looking anxiously and purposefully out of the window at his car. His name is Rupert. For three years he has been living on the other side of the city with his girlfriend, but the relationship has come to an end and he wants somewhere to stay short-term while he looks for a more permanent home. He works long hours for an energy supply company up in town; he needs somewhere to sleep, to hang his suits, to house his television – apparently it's quite large. While he speaks he looks at me fixedly with his small pale eyes, but whenever I reply he looks shyly down and away to the side. With his fine, almost white hair and his downcast eyes he looks either innocent or guilty, I can't tell.

The clocks have gone forward and now the evenings are long and as blank as paper. People stay out late on the streets calling and shouting, music pouring from open windows, cars revving and honking in the dusk. Someone new has moved in next door and erected his sound system on the other side of my bedroom wall. All night the electronic pulses probe and torment the space between us. I wander through the dark house, checking the locks on the doors and windows, for it feels as though the outside is coming in, as though a wall of defence has come down, as though the doors and windows may as well not be there at all. We are a house of women and children, but I wonder whether our vulnerability is anything more than something invented to make men feel brave. When there's a war men go off to it, leaving the women and children behind, and when they return perhaps it is to find that they have made themselves dispensable, like Agamemnon returning to Argos from Troy. I wonder whether we will be safer with Rupert in the house or more at risk. There is a space here, an impression, like a footprint in the sand or a cast, a male declivity in the shape of my husband. Vaguely I try to fit Rupert into it. I imagine him fixing the drains, the door handles, having a look inside the dishwasher to see what's wrong. Man is either protector or predator, I can't quite remember which.

Rupert is efficient with his paperwork, his deposit, his references. He brings his iron and his humorous posters, his suits. He brings his television, which stands on a plinth in his room like a vast black blinking god. I give him two shelves in the fridge and he fills them with ready meals for one, the plastic containers neatly stacked in the cold lit chamber like things in a morgue. My husband comes to collect something while Rupert is in the hall and the two of them shake hands.

'Pleased to meet you,' they both say.

•

Agamemnon, in the *Oresteia* of Aeschylus, returns to his palace in Argos, the victor after ten years' war against the Trojans. He is murdered by his wife Clytemnestra as soon as he sets foot in the hall, walking over the costly crimson tapestries with which she has laid the palace floor as his bitter homecoming tribute. Later she is murdered in her turn by their children, Orestes and Electra, who cannot forgive her for disposing of their father, imperfect though he was.

My children are interested in the ancient Greeks. They have a surprising knowledge of Greek mythology, know its twists and turns, are familiar with its cast of characters. When they talk about it it's as though they are talking about something they personally remember. I suppose this knowledge can only have come from books, so it is memory in a way. For a child a book and a memory can be difficult to tell apart. All the same it's surprising, how much they know. Freud viewed the formation of individual personality as analogous to human history: I like this way of understanding a life, as a re-enactment in miniature of civilisation. According to this analogy the ancient Greeks are the formative phases of infancy, in which the psyche is shaped and given its irrevocable character. So it's fitting, I suppose, that a child should have a special attraction to these tales of gods and mortals, to the joy and anarchy of the early world, in which fantasy and reality have not yet been separated, in which the moral authority of God the father has not yet been asserted and guilt and conscience do not yet exist.

We once visited what is said to be Agamemnon's tomb, on a family holiday in the Peloponnese. It is a vast conical space dug beneath a hot hillside at Mycenae where bees buzz amid the wildflowers, the tomb itself beehive-shaped, as though in acknowledgement of what is really the only immortality, the return of all things human to the eternal substances of nature. Clytemnestra's tomb is there too: the two are far apart, for this is a story not of marriage but of separation, of the attempt to break the form of marriage and be free. There are two tombs, just as there were two people: separation is a demand for space, the expression of the self's need to regain its integrity. The double tomb, like the double bed, symbolises the power of marriage to erase these distinctions. At night I used to wake up and ask myself the question, who am I? For there in the darkness, in the marital bed, I felt myself wheeling on the edge of a black chasm, wheeling with the planets in outer space, hurtling through a blackness rashed with stars. The reality of my room, my home, my life couldn't seem to anchor me. I was frightened of dying, not because I loved life but because I couldn't distinguish myself, couldn't gather together as one entity this self whose existence posited the fact of non-existence. It was like seeing a shadow without being able to see what cast it. I didn't know who I was: yet 'I' would one day die.

On the hot hillside above the tomb I told my children the story of the *Oresteia*, hardly knowing what it was I was telling them. Does Clytemnestra know that Agamemnon is coming home? Is the murder calculated, a plan shaped during the years of his absence, or is it a sudden, unpremeditated explosion of violence? Yes, she knows: she keeps a guard posted day and night on the palace walls as a lookout. She has had bonfires laid on every hillside between Argos and Troy, waiting to be lit in the event of the warriors' return. It is the behaviour of a tyrant, a dictator, this obsessive news-gathering, this round-the-clock surveillance. And indeed this is how Clytemnestra's subjects speak of her, as a kind of Iron Lady, a man in a woman's body. They too watch for those beacons to be lit, signifying victory at Troy and the return of their king. They are uncomfortable with this female version of power. It is a kind of theft, when a woman behaves like a man, or indeed a man like a woman. There is the feeling that someone's been murdered, been done away with in the robbery.

Clytemnestra has had no choice but to live and rule without her husband all these years; a working mother, if you will, single parent to her son Orestes and her daughter Electra. There was another daughter, Iphegenia, the eldest, who is dead. Her absence haunts this drama, this family, for in a way a family and a drama are the same thing. Iphegenia died at the very time her father Agamemnon set sail for Troy: the two events are inseparably linked. On that day, Agamemnon and his fleet, all prepared for war, found themselves becalmed in the harbour and unable to depart. There was no wind to fill the sails: the driving force of civilisation, the whole thrusting work of men caught up in the furtherance of their aims, was brought to a standstill by a simple withdrawal of the favourable conditions. They had forgotten that they depended on this favour, this willingness of the wind. They had forgotten to propitiate Artemis, the goddess whose wind it was, as men forget at their peril to propitiate the women on whose willingness their plans and projects depend, for though women don't fight wars or build civilisation, all is conditional on their willingness for it to be done. Were women not willing, civilisation would be halted. There the men sat in the harbour, armed to the teeth, with no means of getting where they wanted to go. What could they give Artemis to bring her round? How could they mollify her, fast, in order to get going? An extravagant gift was the answer. She liked sacrifices, the blood of virgins, a valuable girl laid on her altar like a cultured pearl. Agamemnon's daughter Iphegenia, a virgin, a princess, and what's more dearly loved by her parents, would make a rare present. Especially the love: the goddess would appreciate that, like the special lustre on the pearl of great price. All night Agamemnon agonised, but as Clytemnestra bitterly noted, what he decided came as no surprise. And what is it, the agony of decision where the decision is already made? Had Agamemnon not agonised, Iphegenia's value would have been diminished. Had he offered her up easily, the goddess might not have been satisfied. The agony was a kind of formality, but it was a perversion too, a misuse of emotion. The next day Iphegenia was led out in the saffron-coloured dress that was meant for her wedding, and lying bound on the stone altar she watched while her father raised a knife and drove it into her heart.

•

Rupert tells me that his girlfriend, once so clinging and dependent, has found a new lease of life in their separation. She has moved up to London; she is out every night, at bars and clubs and parties. He claims to be relieved: he was the one who brought their relationship to an end, and was prepared to do a certain amount of penance for it. He had expected long, tearful telephone calls, flashes of anger and accusation, pleas for reconciliation. But instead, when he speaks to her – which is rarely – she claims to feel liberated. He's worried, though; after all, he knows her well. She's a woman whose sorrows take extrovert and hedonistic forms. Yet the fact is she doesn't seem to need him, doesn't call.

Every day he leaves the house early, at half past six, vanished into the pale light of morning amid the seagulls' cacophonous waking cries. He retires early too, at half past nine. Sometimes I glimpse his male form in the dusky stairwell, clad in a white towelling robe. In the kitchen his ready meals revolve in the planetary light of the microwave oven. He eats on a stool at the counter, turning the pages of a newspaper. Once a month he has a Saturday off and takes his mother out to lunch: she lives not far away. Rupert is her only child; his father left when he was a baby and started a new family elsewhere. His second wife is rich and powerful where Rupert's mother is fragile and impoverished. He hasn't seen his father for years. The two of them have moved around the country, drifting like dandelion seeds troubled by breezes, too light and bewildered to find the earth. For a while Rupert attended a choir school. Despite the insubstantiality of his origins, he was discovered to have a strong voice. The school was an upper-class institution: Rupert was given a scholarship. When he speaks of that time he wears a child's costive expression on his face. The choristers would sing in their white robes from the top of the bell tower. One day one of Rupert's schoolfellows climbed the tower and jumped off it. I ask whether he still sings and he screws up his mouth in reply.

•

Agamemnon hesitates before treading the tapestries underfoot and entering the palace, just as Adam hesitated before taking the red apple Eve held out to him. Woman, it seems, does not suffer these qualms. She is not afraid, or else she is in the grip of something stronger than fear, stronger than obedience. Clytemnestra persuades Agamemnon, as Eve persuaded Adam. She alludes to the splendour and beauty of the tapestries, their costliness, his might in walking over them; Agamemnon is torn, torn between obedience to the gods and the desire to submit to his wife. It is as though, for a man, a woman represents the possibility of doing without God. She is a force of pure mortality, in whom the darkest and richest possibilities for living can be realised. Who are her gods? Whose authority, in the end, does she herself recognise?

He walks in, walks over the tapestries. He treads their beauty underfoot and she kills him. What does it signify, her need to get him inside? In a marriage, inside is where intimacy happens, where couples fight or make love, where they're honest, where they're their 'real' selves. Most marriages have a public face, an aspect of performance, like the body has its skin. A couple arguing in public is like the body bleeding, but there are other forms of death that aren't apparent on the outside. People are shocked by cancer, so noiseless and invisible, and by the break-up of couples whose hostility to one another never showed. They seemed so happy, people say, for the idea that death might give no sign of its coming leads us to suspect it is already here. You were the last people, a close friend said to me, the last people we expected this to happen to. And this friend, like some others, went away, just as people run away from plague victims in their agony, for fear that it might be catching. Sometimes the phone rings in my half-empty house and a woman's voice says, we're so sorry. We were so sorry to hear.

Clytemnestra, in her husband's ten-year absence, has become intimate with Aegysthus. He is not, of course, the father of her children. He is not her husband, for her husband still lives. She is queen of Argos but Aegysthus cannot be king alongside her, for the king – her husband, Agamemnon – still lives. There is no space for Aegysthus, no throne, no room. If Agamemnon were dead a space would be created: the fatherless children, the husbandless wife, the country with no king, these would be vacuums that needed filling to keep the enterprise of life afloat. But as it stands, despite Clytemnestra's will, nothing about Aegysthus meets with a fair wind.

His authority is rejected everywhere: the children resent him, the people refuse to recognise him, the country is viewed as being in a terrible plight. In marriage Clytemnestra found the force of life came up effortless and strong; children were born, power accrued, ambitions took root and flourished, but most of all there was belief, belief in the rightness and reality of it all. It is interesting what people will forgive, what they will tolerate, when they believe. When they doubt they will tolerate nothing, and Aegysthus is doubted by everyone except the woman Clytemnestra.

In Agamemnon's absence Clytemnestra has had to play his role: she has learned that she is capable of governing his palace, of ruling Argos, of commanding his underlings. So the mystery of his masculinity has been, to an extent, unveiled; the form of male and female has been tested and found to be limitation and lie. This new relationship with Aegysthus has been chosen by the new unisexual Clytemnestra. She is seeking a new form, a new configuration of female and male. She is seeking equality. Children will not be born from equality, nor will empires be built or frontiers expanded, for the pure peace of equality begets nothing. It is all aftermath, predicated on the death of what was before. To beget requires the domination of one thing by the other, the domination of female form by male content; then, in order to nurture what has been begotten, the reverse. Clytemnestra wants no more begetting. She wants the peace of equality but to get it she will have to use violence. To reach aftermath, first there has to be the event itself.

Why does she hate him so, this heroic husband of hers? Would she hate Aegysthus too if he were her bonded mate, father of her children, captain and gatekeeper of her life's enterprise? Do all women have a special capacity to hate their husbands, all husbands

the capacity to hate their wives with a hatred that is somewhere
fused with the very origins of life? The first time I saw my husband
after our separation I realised, to my surprise, that he hated me. I
had never seen him hate anyone: it was as though he was filled up
with something that was not of himself, contaminated by it, like a
coastline painted black by an oil spill. For months black poisonous
hatred has flowed from the fatal wound to our marriage, flowed
through every source and outlet, soaked into everything, coated the
children like the downy heads of coastal birds are coated in tar. I
remember how towards the end it felt like a dam giving way by
degrees, the loss of courtesy and caution, the breakdown of civility
and self-control: these defences seemed to define the formal core of
marriage, of relationship, to articulate the separation of one person
from another. Without them we would lose our form. Form is both
safety and imprisonment, both protector and dissembler: form, in
the end, conceals truth, just as the body conceals the cancer that
will destroy it. Form is rigid, inviolable, devastatingly correct; that
is its vulnerability. Form can be broken. It will tolerate variation
but not transgression; it can be broken, but at what cost? If it is
destroyed what can be put in its place? The only alternative to form
is chaos.

An outcast from marriage, I look at other marriages with a
different eye. Silently I congratulate the couples I pass in the street,
while at the same time wondering why they are together and I am
alone. I know that they have succeeded where I have failed, yet I
can't seem to remember why this is so. Later in the *Oresteia*, when
Clytemnestra has herself been murdered, the Furies tasked with
representing her female outrage and keeping her righteous anger
alive in the world keep falling asleep. They become drowsy, lazy,

forgetful: they fail to remember and articulate the injustice she has suffered in her attempt to be free, to pursue the murderer and be his conscience, to keep cleaning the black tar of hate from her image. And I, too, cannot remember what drove me to destroy the life I had. All I know is that it is lost, gone. The blackness of hate flows and flows over me, unimpeded. I let it come. I cannot remember.

But Agamemnon killed Clytemnestra's daughter, her first child. Men are said to resent the child that first takes the woman's love and attention away. And it is true that a woman can find relief in loving something that is not her opposite. Her baby doesn't judge her, doesn't desire her: for a while it seems to reconnect her with her own childlikeness, her girlishness, her innocence, but in reality her links to that state have been irrevocably severed by motherhood. The baby can seem like something her husband has given her as a substitute for himself, a kind of transitional object, like a doll, for her to hold so that he can return to the world. And he does, he leaves her, returning to work, setting sail for Troy. He is free, for in the baby the romance of man and woman has been concluded: each can now do without the other. Out of their love they created an object, the baby, and in doing so they defined it, defined their love and its limitations.

Their romance has been concluded and now, perhaps, they are murderously angry with one another. Perhaps she thought the baby would make him love her more, but in fact she seems to have lost him: he has used it, the baby, to make his escape from her. She doesn't want a doll after all – she wants a man, a man to love her and desire her. Iphegenia, led out in her saffron-coloured wedding dress, is perhaps the sacrifice that lies at the heart of all marriages, the death on which the whole enterprise is built.

•

Everywhere I see couples, but when I get close enough to hear them the impression changes. Image becomes reality: I am briefly entangled in the net of marital conversation as it passes, am momentarily webbed in its tensions and politics, its million-threaded illusion of harmony. When couples talk, everything they say means something else. Their talk is referential, but the reality it refers to is hidden from view. You see the shadow, but not the object that casts it.

Most evenings now Rupert and I meet in the kitchen. He is always in: I go downstairs and there he is. It is the opposite of marriage, this endlessly recurring randomness through which we find ourselves thrown together. While his supper revolves we talk. He asks me about my situation. He's interested in the house and in the nature of its energy supply. One evening he opens a bottle of wine and offers me a glass. He offers me a share of his meal, pasta with a red sauce that comes from a Heinz jar. He says he thinks he can arrange a cheaper deal for me, if I give him all the paperwork. He loosens his tie. Outside the kitchen windows is a dry, violet-coloured darkness, and from the neighbouring gardens comes the sound of people talking and laughing in the warm evening. In my garden cats prowl through the overgrown grass and recently I saw a huge fox, mangy and ruddy, standing on the back wall on its four cankered legs in the dusk. Upstairs the children lie asleep in their beds: I imagine them there, like people sleeping in the cabin of a ship that has sailed off its course, unconscious of the danger they're in. We have lost our bearings, lost our history, and I am the ship's captain, standing full of dread at the helm. Rupert sloshes more wine into our glasses. He tells me I'm doing a great job. He tells me he thinks I'm a very nice person. He tells me we're in the same boat, in a way. After a while I say goodnight, and go and shut myself in my room.

I book our summer holiday, the same holiday we always take, to a much-loved familiar place. I tell my husband that we can split the holiday in half, changing over like runners in a relay race, passing the baton of the children. He refuses. He says he will never go to that place again. He wants only what is unknown to him, what is unfamiliar. He thinks there is something ruthless and strange in my intention to revisit a place where once we were together, and the truth is I don't yet realise the pain this intention will cost me, the discipline I will have to inculcate to endure it. Great if it doesn't bother you, he says. I say, you want to deny our shared history. You want to pretend our family never happened. That's about right, he says. I say, I don't see why the children should lose everything that made them happy. Great, he says. Good for you.

Rupert is gone in the mornings by the time I get the children up for school, and in the evenings I avoid him. I stay in my room, fencing with the long nights. I can no longer sleep: I'm too frightened of dreaming, and of waking from the dreams. I'm frightened of my house. I'm frightened of my own bed. I feel as though I have walked out into a world that looked through the windows to be balmy and warm, only to discover that the sun was the frozen sun of winter, the dazzling light that of polar regions and glaciers. It is colder out here than I could ever have imagined.

One night I hear the front door violently slam: Rupert has gone out. He does not return until the next morning. He does not go to work. All day I am aware of him in his room. At nightfall he emerges in his white robe, ill-looking and sheepish. He says he called in sick; he overdid it a bit last night, at the pubs and clubs in the town centre. Did he go out with friends? Well, no, not exactly, though he seems to remember meeting a few people in the course of things. But no, he went out drinking alone. He came back at about three and slept the rest of the night in his car. He's been sleeping most of the day, but he's a bit the worse for wear. He looks at me dartingly, his eyes yellow with drink.

I go away for a few days with the children and when I return my neighbour calls round. There's been a disturbance, she says. She hates to have to tell me. Your lodger, she says. She says she's written to him threatening the police if it goes on. She hopes I don't mind her doing that, but she was really at her wits' end. He was out there, she says, pointing. Out there in the garden. It was gone midnight and she had gone to bed, when she heard the most excruciating, demoniacal noise. She got up; other people began to open their windows and call down, and eventually she opened her window too. There he was on the lawn in the darkness, wearing nothing but his boxer shorts. She said to him, people are trying to sleep and you're making the most dreadful noise. You're creating a disturbance. But he didn't seem to hear; he didn't really seem to know she was there. The next day she came and rang on the bell. She said she hoped there would be no more nonsense, and he agreed that there wouldn't. But then there he was again, the next night. He started at about one and it went on until five or six in the morning, out in the garden with not a stitch on. But it was the noise, this simply awful noise he made, on and on and on until she thought she'd go mad.

What sort of noise? I said. What was he doing?

Well it's funny, she said, but I think he was trying to sing.

•

In the biblical story, Abraham also binds his child to an altar and raises a knife over his head. At least Isaac remains ignorant as he's led up the mountainside of what his fate is to be. Abraham, like a good father, tells him a half lie: he makes out that they are going up there to sacrifice a lamb. Is it because there's nothing in this for him that Abraham is capable of that small act of mercy? His sacrifice won't oil the wheels of civilisation; he isn't doing it to make the wind blow, to turn things his way. His God has merely required it of him, with the cruelty that can only be born of intimacy, for God knows that Abraham cherishes Isaac more than anything else. Recently Abraham criticised God for his plan to lay waste the iniquitous cities of Sodom and Gomorrah, killing the righteous side by side with the sinners, for there is always good to be found even where evil has the upper hand, and why, Abraham wanted to know, should people who had struggled to resist evil receive the same punishment as those who had succumbed to it? In reply God merely thundered at him for having the temerity to hold an opinion, like a parent thundering at an inquisitive child. Now God retaliates by directing Abraham to destroy what he loves the most. He is teaching him a lesson, for isn't that precisely how God feels about the prospect of destroying those righteous residents of irredeemable Sodom? It's hard to be God, hard to be responsible, to be in charge: that's the lesson here, that responsibility means putting moral duty above personal feeling. If Agamemnon's was a lesson in the harsh politics of self-interest, in the suppression of feeling as a winning move in the pursuit of success and the human power play with the gods, then Abraham's is precisely the reverse. It's a lesson in the discipline of objectivity, a discipline that is nowhere more exacting than in its governing of the moral core of love.

Unlike Artemis, this Christian God is satisfied by willingness: Abraham binds his terrified child to the altar and raises the knife, and at that moment God sends an angel to stay his hand. Blood no longer has any value, in this new world of ideas. Justice has become cerebral, logical, academic. But I imagine Abraham and Isaac walking back down the mountainside afterwards in silence, their story of love in tatters. The father has learned that he is capable of harming his child. The child has learned that parental love is not the safety he believed it to be. What will the new story be, grown from this terrible knowledge?

DARK WINDOWS

My daughters and I do not leave home very often: a kind of numbness has settled on our household that any movement can transform into pain. For a while I thought that going elsewhere created possibilities of consolation, even of recovery, but I have discovered that every welcome is also a form of exposure. It is as though, in other people's houses, we become aware of our own nakedness. At one time I mistook this nakedness for freedom, but I don't any more.

It is my mother's seventieth birthday party, a high occasion: everyone is there. The driveway of my brother's house is crammed with cars. We too came by car, along the motorway and then on smaller roads that took us through countryside and villages, little redbrick places that reminded me of the village where I used to visit my grandmother as a child. We lived in America then, and that English village, so damp and miniature-seeming, so full of twists and turns and cavities, constituted my education in the country of my parents, where soon I would come to live for good. In California I wasn't quite sure who I was: large pieces of the jigsaw were missing, and it seemed that the missing pieces were here, in this twisting rain-darkened place. I half-recognised them, the antiquity and the expressive weather, the hedgerows with their mysterious

convoluted interiors, the sense of a solid provenance that underlay
the surface movements of life like wood beneath the burnish: they
were part of me and yet they lay outside me. It was difficult to say –
to prove – that they were mine. In the gas-smelling kitchen, rain at
the windows, my grandmother buttered the cut face of the cottage
loaf before she sliced it, and I watched her like a savage observing
a missionary, or perhaps it was the other way around. Either way, I
was an onlooker, though I didn't want to be. I wanted to live in the
moment instead of always being lifted out of it into awareness, like
a child lifted out of its warm bed half-asleep in the thick of night.

But awareness was the consequence and the curse of that divided life. I couldn't help noticing England more perhaps than the
people who lived there, just as now I notice the unbroken home,
the unified lives that I see through lit windows. When I lived behind those windows I wondered about what was outside. Now that
division has been externalised again, has become actual, like the
geographical division of my youth. I am no longer a participant:
once more, I am an observer. To observe is not to not feel – in fact
it is to put yourself at the mercy of feeling, like the child's warm
skin meeting the cold air of midnight. My own children, too, have
been roused from the unconsciousness of childhood; theirs too is
the pain and the gift of awareness. 'I have two homes,' my daughter
said to me one evening, clearly and carefully, 'and I have no home.'
To suffer and to know what it is that you suffer: how can that be
measured against its much-prized opposite, the ability to be happy
without knowing why?

A white limousine pulls out of a junction into the road in front
of us, a wedding car, as stately as a hearse. Through its darkened
windows I see a lattice of white ribbons; I see the empty back seat,

all decked with arrangements of waxy pale flowers. I see the driver in cap and uniform, staring straight ahead. His solemnity, his self-importance, are striking. In his role as functionary to the eternal rites, he seems to make no distinction between life and death. I wonder whether he is on his way to discharge his duties, or returning from them. In the back of our own car is an enormous cake. I baked it the day before, in one of those vague states that sometimes descend on me now, where a slight uncoupling from reality occurs: I seem to skate or float down an incline of time, and only realise I can't steer or stop when something concrete and hazardous appears in my path. There is at first a consumptive glamour to suffering, for suffering is the corollary of health just as drunkenness is of sobriety. It is the move away from normality that is glamorous. A veil is torn down – how delirious it is, how curiously liberating, to tear it! For a while the old state lends its light to the new, like the sun lending light to a whirling dead star, but gradually I have become conscious of a vast cold, a silence, advancing across it like a shadow. I see the magnitude of the suffering in the same instant as I understand that I can no longer avoid it. It is frightening then to be stranded in that delirium, like the drunk for whom sobriety is as inaccessible as a locked house to which the keys have been mislaid. You can try the handle, look in through the dark windows, but you can't get inside.

The cake is a three-tiered cake, the tiers cemented and then the whole edifice plastered from top to bottom with icing. The children decorated it, with hard little icing rosebuds and silver balls that came from a packet. In different-coloured icing they wrote 'Happy Birthday' on the top. The cake is so large that it has to travel in an enormous cardboard box. I keep glimpsing its summit in the rear-view mirror, a gaudy mountain. It seems both cheap and extravagant: from the back of the car it emanates waves of grandiosity and shame. I realise that the cake is a failure. There was something fanciful in my conception of it that was somehow allowed to run riot, unconstrained by a proper recognition of the labour involved in bringing it to life. My vision – three different tiers of lemon, chocolate and vanilla – had become detached from my competence. I remember from childhood how easy it was to imagine, how hard to create: the difference between what I could conceive of and what I could actually do was bewildering. In adulthood I have learned that to envisage is nothing: success is a hard currency, earned by actual excellence. The vision has to be externalised, and in the case of the cake it remains the prisoner of my imaginings. Dimly I recall my hours in the kitchen the day before, mixing and baking the different tiers. I didn't use a recipe: utterly at the service of my vision, I was operating by blind faith alone. Yet I was neglectful, careless, not measuring things properly, taking shortcuts wherever I could. Was it because the vision was mine that I was so careless with it? I see the same impatience sometimes when my children undertake something they can't execute, a sort of disregard – almost a contempt – for practicality, perhaps even for reality itself. What they like is what is in their heads – how boring it is, how hard and intransigent, this plane on which their imaginings aren't recognised, where their visions are translated into shapeless nonsensical things! I too forgot, during those hours, the hard standard of success; forgot that people would be eating this cake, judging it. When the tiers were cooked I removed them from their tins, three rubbery discs whose indeterminate colour and smell I apprehended from a great psychological distance. I buried them in icing, as though burying the product of my shame; and the children decorated the mound with flowers and inscriptions like a freshly dug grave. Children have a knack for the funereal, a certain authority where death is concerned. Unlike their creativity, this is pure competence. It looks nice, Mummy, they both said, as we interred it in its cardboard box.

My family requires several tables laid end to end to accommodate it. In my brother's house the biggest room has been cleared to make way. The tables have been brought in, amassed from all over: the dining-room table and the kitchen table, the leaf-strewn garden table, desks and side tables from around the house, and lastly a huge piece of chipboard laid across two trestles carried over from the garage. It is autumn, a cold bright Sunday, and the light comes without warmth through the sitting-room windows. The different tables stand in a long line, their ends touching in the hard light. My sister-in-law unfolds an enormous tablecloth: it is two cloths, in fact, of the same material, with a runner laid across the centre to hide the join. As she spreads them out the oddity of different surfaces, the cheap beside the costly, the jigsaw of inadequacy and splendour, is transformed into a vision of wholeness. No one would now guess at the compromise that lies beneath the smart tablecloths; the fact that the underlying structure is both less and more than it seems has been lost to the conformity of the surface.

The youngest person sitting down to lunch is two, the oldest – my grandmother – ninety-two. There has never been a divorce in this clan. Some children are the first in their family history to go to university: mine are the first to experience the public breakdown of their parents' marriage. Other than myself, of the many assembled adults only my grandmother is without her mate. My grandfather died when my grandmother was in her sixties: for nearly thirty years she has lived without a husband. These three decades begin to rival the decades of her marriage like the outskirts of a town engulfing its historic centre, yet that centre holds, remains the explanation, the cause. Unlike me, my grandmother never ended the story; it goes on, with or without certain of its main characters.

When I was younger I thought she must be relieved to be alone, after all those years. Though I had loved my grandfather I saw it as a disencumbrance, a liberation, like taking off shoes that hurt. Marriage appeared to me as a holding-in, a corseting, and it seemed to my eyes that the force of constraint was male; that it was men who imposed this structure, marriage, in order to make a woman unavailable, and with her the gifts of love and warmth that otherwise might have flowed freely out into the world. But men provided shelter, and money: I understood that a woman could not merely liberate herself, couldn't just take herself off with her gifts of love and warmth and go elsewhere. What had happened to my grandmother seemed the ideal solution, to be left with the chattels but freed from the male authority that had provided them, though admittedly it had taken an awfully long time to happen. It never occurred to me that she might remarry, might enter again into that bondage, and indeed she never did. And it never occurred to me either that she might have remained alone out of loyalty to the familial enterprise; that she might have been lonely, have sickened for companionship, but continued to play her part for the sake of her children; that she might have understood, as I did not, that the jigsaw is frail, not strong, is a mirage, not a prison. It is not to dismantle but to conserve it that strength is required, for it will come apart in an instant. It will come apart, that image, and what remains is not a new or different image but a pile of pieces that mean nothing at all.

At the end of lunch the enormous cake is brought in, amid exclamations in which I believe I can detect notes of uncertainty. For a moment the threat – or rather the knowledge – of failure is unbearable, the inescapable knowledge that is the essence of this second life, this aftermath. As a child, I read the book of life through the adults I knew, just as now I read it through my children, the second reading perhaps a form of atonement for the first, for I know what it is to be a child. That first reading was savage and revelatory where the second is empathetic and philosophical: eyes strained against the darkness of my own ignorance, I struggled to comprehend the grandeur and violence of the adult world, to grasp its double nature of seeming and being. And in this duplicity, this difference between how things looked and what they were, was something to which I couldn't be reconciled, just as now I can't forget that under the pretty tablecloths lies a makeshift structure that has no form or beauty of its own. In much the same way, I saw the romance of marriage as a covering for something unapologetically practical, saw it as the metaphor for woman, the beautiful creature who cooks and cleans. Why couldn't the outside and the inside be the same? Beneath the surface of my cake is something worse than practical, worse than makeshift: it is the reversal of meaning; it is failure itself. Far better to be practical than to make a foul-tasting cake. Better to go to a shop and buy a cake than to produce this extravagant travesty of love.

The first Christmas after my grandfather died, my grandmother cried at the table, a paper hat from a Christmas cracker on her head. I remember the way the flimsy hat sat jauntily on her greying hair as she wept. It seemed to readmit her to the world of childhood; and indeed I sensed around the table a slight impatience with her conduct to which my own frequent emotional outbursts had long since accustomed me. For some reason her tears were not permitted: the obligation to romanticise marriage had been, somehow, reversed by my grandfather's absence. The covers were off: why on earth was she trying to put them back on again? My grandmother had been brave in marriage: for more than forty years the surface was maintained. It seemed unfair that she shouldn't be allowed to sentimentalise now, when it could do no harm. In her jaunty hat, husbandless, she had been returned to the caste and strictures of childhood, to our end of the table, where people were told when they could and couldn't cry.

There is no crying now, at my mother's birthday party. I look around at my family as though through a million-splintered pane of glass. The world on my side of the glass is as white and cold and silent as an Arctic plain. A song is sung; the cake is cut and cut, divided and redivided into numberless sections. I feel a certain relief at its dismantling, but a cake is not a jigsaw. Its character survives: no matter how finely you cut it, each section replicates the strata of the whole. A piece is put in front of me, my portion, but the others take their portions too. I watch the plates go around the table. I am inflicting failure on my family, or else they are relieving me of it. We lift our glasses in a toast. My mother tells me to eat: she can see my bones. My father says he thinks my driving has improved since I've been on my own. My grandmother pats my hand. Mark my words, she says, you two will make it up. Just you wait and see.

•

My sister comes to stay and we take our children to the park. It is a grey weeping Sunday afternoon. In the greyness the colours hurt, the red of passing buses, the yellow vests of men drilling in the road nearby, the drab fluorescent pink and blue of children's bicycles passing on the tarmac paths. The grass is sodden underfoot. I watch the people, the mothers with their buggies, the old men standing while their dogs sniff at the verges, the fathers in sports clothes kicking balls in the drizzle, the children roaming the fenced playground with a kind of stillborn exhilaration, like animals in captivity. We take the children to the swings. I watch my daughters: sometimes, when I look at them, it is as though they are wearing masks. Their faces take on the immobility of representation, like the white masks of antiquity with their downturned mouths, though quite what they are representing – their own unhappiness or mine – I am not sure. Either way, something that should be hidden is suddenly visible. The unselfconsciousness of childhood is reversed: they are children turned inside out.

When it starts to rain we leave the park and walk through the leafy Victorian streets of this neighbourhood, which is not my own. I have been thinking I might move over here, away from the disturbances of the sea; might move away from the strain of ceaseless change, the heaving water always so naked, so abandoned, rolling in darkness and light. I imagine a home here, in this redbrick clamp of streets, imagine it as safe and faintly purgatorial, a continuing sameness in which my sins will not devour me but will be dutifully paid off over a lifetime in small increments, like a mortgage. It is the annual weekend where the city's artists open their houses to show the public their work, and when we pass one we go inside, out of the rain. On the walls there are framed photographs, watercolours, oil paintings; further in there are racks of handmade postcards, and prints stacked up in cellophane wrappers on a table.

Again and again their subject is the sea. Here it is in its stormy mood, and there in its benign; here a sheet of empty glare, there a broken surface releasing light. We see it with and without sailing boats, at dawn and dusk, peopled and deserted, wintry, balmy and dull. There are pictures of seaweed, of driftwood, of the pebbles on the beach. There are pictures of the painted huts that line the esplanade: they remind me of the lined-up saints that surround early Renaissance portraits of the Madonna, for in its devotion and repetition this too is a display of religious iconography, its goddess the ocean. In these streets there is no sight or atmosphere of the sea: this could be a pleasant neighbourhood in any landlocked town. There is something obsessive, something almost fetishistic in these images, preoccupied as they are with what is absent, or rather with what is just out of reach. I mistrust this exposure of that which already exposes itself, the naked sea; the mind feeding off its dramas from the safety of the suburb. Yet I imagine moving here, and hanging a picture of the sea on my wall. It has been my belief that the only way to know something is to experience it, that the truest forms of knowledge are personal. Now I imagine a different kind of knowledge, knowledge without exposure, without risk; the knowledge of the voyeur, watching, assessing, staying hidden.

The children tug at our sleeves: they are bored, and want to go. Outside we continue along the rainy pavements. Water drips from the trees. At the end of the road there is another open house, and the children run ahead and disappear inside. We follow, and find ourselves in a front garden as fanciful as a fairy tale, full of chiming bells and odd little creatures made of clay. Behind it stands a house deep in its gloom of trees. It has stained-glass windows and gables scalloped like the hair of an eccentric milkmaid. The door is open: inside all is sepia, and rich with dust. We pass through the hall and into a large disorderly room that is full of a strange, jewelled light. Though it is sullen and grey outside, the stained-glass windows cast their coloured oblongs inward. A lady stands at a large table, with the windows at her back. She is extremely tall, with long fair plaits. In front of her, on the table, are a number of curious hats or headdresses; and standing at the table are the children, who as we enter turn around. One of my daughters has become a stag, with dark branching antlers; the other a fox, with a long russet nose and a velvety head. My little niece has become a fieldmouse, my nephew a badger with a bushy white crest. They look at us with dark glossy eyes through the tinted light. In the few minutes of our absence they have been transformed: they are creatures startled in a forest glade by the approach of danger. The lady, too, is satisfied by the drama of their appearance. She makes the masks herself, she tells us: they are designed for adults, but they look much more lifelike on children. She herself likes to wear the stag, though it does make her terribly tall.

Presently the children take the masks off, all except the stag, whose fondness for hers has perhaps been intensified by hearing that its owner has a special fondness for it too. Can I have it? she asks me. Will you buy it for me? She says this from within the face of the stag, for I can't see her mouth. The mask is richly made, beautifully heavy and padded: its transformation of her is complete, yet it seems too to have accommodated her own nature, so that I find I'm already quite used to her looking like that. In a strange way we are both relieved by her metamorphosis. The lady tells me the price. It is high, but not as much as I expected. My stag-daughter watches me, alert, bright-eyed, perfectly still. Please, she says. Please, I love it.

Everyone waits to see what I will do, my niece and nephew, my daughters, my sister, the tall lady with the fair plaits. They sense a vacuum of authority. How is it possible that we set out for a walk in the park and have ended up embroiled in the purchase of a bohemian headdress? The only certainty I can locate in myself is that of my desire to undermine authority itself. Authority would refuse her the mask because of the randomness of her request for it. Authority would not allow itself to be led by a course of events. Yet I myself am now authority. And so although I want to buy her the mask, though I know she would love it and value it, though it is entirely up to me, what I decide to say to her is no. But before I can, she lifts the mask from her head. Her face is revealed again, flushed, a little dishevelled. She sets it carefully back on the table. I don't need it, she says. Don't worry. I've changed my mind.

•

Later, at the train station before she leaves, my sister says to me: you have to learn to hide what you feel from the children. They will feel what they think you feel. They are only reflections of you.

I don't believe that, I say.

If they think you're happy, they'll be happy, my sister says.

Their feelings are their own, I say.

What I feel is that I have jumped from a high place, thinking I could fly, and after a few whirling instants have realised I am simply falling. What I feel is the hurtling approach of disaster. And I have believed they were falling with me, my daughters; I have believed I was looking into their hearts, into their souls, and seen terror and despair there. Is it possible that my children are not windows but mirrors? That what I have seen is my own fall, my own terror, not theirs?

I don't believe that, I say again.

You have to believe it, she says.

On the walk back from the station the rain stops. The sun gushes, metallic and rich, through the rending clouds. A fresh wind comes gusting up the streets after their cleansing. A feeling of freedom grips me and whirls me around, the feeling that I need recognise no authority, need serve no greater structure, that I can do as I like. It will go away again, this feeling, I know, but for now it is here. I pass slumbrous houses, a locked church, a little tattoo parlour whose shopfront is obscured by sinuous images of snakes and flowers. I pass a restaurant and through its big windows see a family sitting at a table, the mother rising and reaching across to give something to the baby in its high chair. I can smell food, hear the clatter of dishes and the sound of people talking in the kitchen. A man in a chef's apron is standing at a side door, smoking in the sunshine. He is only a few feet away from them but the family can't see him: they are inside in the dining room, at a table spread with a white cloth. Through the window I can see the remains of their meal, the wreckage of cutlery and crumpled napkins and dirty plates, the broken crusts of bread lying against the white. A few minutes ago, when the rain was pouring down, they must have felt fortunate to be safe and dry inside, inside where everything exists to serve them. The woman holds her reaching stance: I watch her pale transverse form through the glass. She is like a statue, frozen in the moment of her motherhood, reaching across to her child. Her husband sits erect, looking straight ahead, as though something outside has caught his attention. It is as though, in that instant, he has seen the restaurant's servitude become a trap: he looks across her leaning shape, looks out through the dark windows at the lifting day outside, the gold gushing sunshine, the freedom and freshness of the street. The man in the chef's apron finishes his cigarette and goes back in. I pass on, thinking about the stag mask with its sweetly farouche expression; about my daughter's heavy branched head turning on her delicate shoulders, about the strange relief I felt at having her masked and at the animal form she took, innocent of human pain. In that guise she could run as fast and as far as she liked to dodge the hunter's arrows. She was free.

AREN'T YOU HAVING ANY?

I have a friend I'm too frightened to see. We used to be close, but when she calls during the smashed days of late summer I shrink from the sound of her voice. I read a story about a woman whose dead grandmother keeps calling the house, leaving long messages on the answering machine in which she bewails her purgatorial loneliness. The woman was fond of her grandmother but eventually she becomes angry, pitiless, shouting down the phone at the dead woman to go away. The calls are making her feel guilty.

My friend lives with her two daughters in a town about an hour from here, in a house an estate agent would describe as 'deceptive'. From the outside it appears tiny: the deception lies in the fact that once the scale of the street has been removed, everything inside is at least in proportion to everything else. My friend is tiny herself, with child-sized hands whose bitten nails she hides in the long sleeves of her too-big jumpers. Once she lived in London with her husband, in a grand establishment where dinner parties were held from which one would come away feeling lacerated, as though the evening had contained a hidden blade that nicked the skin unnoticed. That blade, I suppose, was the animosity between man and wife that later dismembered their household and whole way of life so brutally. The husband met another woman, had new children, bought another grand house to replace the first; and my friend and her daughters were cut away, like the excess cloth fallen from a seamstress's table that the pattern doesn't require.

She moved to this cheaper, less fashionable location, got a job that fitted round her children's school day, gave up drinking, took up yoga. She sees different people, has new opinions, a new haircut. Everything in her doll's house is dainty and white and fresh. It is as though, in the absence of man, woman seizes the opportunity to recover her innocence, to make her world virginal again, to cleanse herself of the gore of sexuality and perfect her femininity. For a while I cleaned my own house incessantly, a maternal Lady Macbeth seeing bloodstains everywhere. The messy cupboards and cluttered shelves were like an actual subconscious I could purge of its guilt and pain. In those cupboards our family still existed, man and woman still mingled, children were still interleaved with their parents, intimacy survived. One day I took everything out and threw it away.

So I'm frightened of my friend. I don't return her calls. Her existence is virtuous, honourable, yet the thought of it paralyses me with terror.

•

My daughter comes back from a school trip with a long face. I ask her how it was. It was all right, she says.

All evening she is quiet, but once she's in bed, the covers pulled up to her chin, she begins to speak. The trip was to a local nature reserve, a place I know, the broad estuary banked by desolate wetlands and marshes. They were there all day. They were asked to choose partners, and each pair was given maps and information packs and questionnaires with which to negotiate their own way around. They were asked to make a note of birds and animals they saw, and to sketch the different wildflowers and grasses. It sounds like fun, I say. Well it was, she says, I mean it would have been. That's what makes it so hard, she says, the fact that it would have been fun.

When the class chose their partners, standing in the car park beside the coach that had brought them there, the group was an odd number and my daughter found herself left out. I ask why she wasn't in a pair with H, her longtime best friend. H chose someone else, she says. It seems that she and H are no longer friends, and that my daughter has been slower than H to make new alliances. I don't blame her, she says. It's not her fault. I'd probably have done exactly the same thing. But all day I had to go around on my own. And it was such a long day, she says, and so much walking and so many things we had to do. The teacher was meant to be her partner but it didn't really work out like that. She kept having to go and help other people, and my daughter kept finding herself alone again.

I didn't realise, I say, about you and H. You didn't tell me.

It's just as much my fault as hers, my daughter says.

What happened? I say.

My daughter shrugs.

She didn't like it when I talked to other people, she says. I wanted to be her friend but I wanted to have other friends too. And she wanted it to be just us.

•

In the mirror my daughters and I look at ourselves. They are growing, getting bigger, and I am shrinking. I can't eat, like a love-
sick girl. But I am not a girl and this is grief. It is the opposite of
excitement.

In the mirror their faces are young and strong and richly coloured, yet blunt and half-formed, full of the unknown, of sentences
not yet uttered. Their heads reach my shoulder. I stand between
them, recessed, shadowy, a creature concealed in the foliage of their
girlish vigour. I feel I could stay hidden like this forever, hidden
in this virginal life with my daughters, but then the image breaks
apart; time resumes; they vanish from the mirror to do other things
and I am left there, as though holding the long and close-typed
book of myself in my hands.

Grief is not love but it is like love. This is romance's estranged
cousin, a cruel character, all sleeplessness and adrenalin unsweet-
ened by hope. I have cousins I have rarely seen, for our families
did not get on: they were like us but they were not us. A few years
ago I saw them at a funeral, grown up now, a group of white-faced
strangers clad in black. We spoke, politely, and it was unnerving
to see in these strangers the lineaments of my siblings' faces; to see
coolness in their expressions instead of warmth, indifference where
usually there was interest, to feel the lack of meaning and connec-
tion in what looked, nonetheless, like intimacy. And grief is somehow the same, resembling what it negates, each cousinly attribute a
denial instead of a reinforcement.

I can't eat, and soon my clothes are too big for me, all gaping
sleeves and sagging waistbands, everything seeming to be on a different scale from myself, just as my mother's clothes were when long
ago I opened her wardrobe and curiously tried them on. In a way

I enjoy the feeling of becoming a child again. It seems to acquit me of men and marriage, this loss of substance; to pair me with my daughters, as though I were rejoining them on the other side of what created them. I feel safer this way. I look at people eating, at restaurant tables, in cafes and on park benches, and compared to them I feel protected, as though what they are ingesting in all its richness and density is compromise. To need is to be compromised. They seem almost vulnerable while they eat.

As a family we would eat around the kitchen table, but now I carry my daughters their supper on a tray. The table is covered in papers and books and electricity bills. I try to remember what our family meals were like, and though the detail escapes me I remember it as a kind of tree, nourishment, with all of us fastened to its branches, as indistinguishable as fruit. Ours was a communal body: there was no individual drama of growing or shrinking. That same tree existed in my childhood, its cycles by turns reassuring and tyrannical. One could break away from it but the tree still stood. As a teenager trying to escape family mealtimes, I remember my mother's disapproval – almost, her fear – of such absences. There was something she wanted us to believe, something she feared we might find out the truth of if we went elsewhere. That there were other places we could eat, perhaps; that this tree, family, was not the only source of life. To reject her food was to reject her; perhaps she thought food was the only thing we really needed from her, or the only thing she could provide. Mealtimes had the religiosity and infallibility of an institution, until we stopped believing in them and they were revealed to be just my mother, providing or needing, it wasn't clear which.

Aren't you having any? my daughters ask me. They are anxious, just like my mother was, but for the opposite reason. As a teenager I felt lumpish and slow, weighted down: I was in no danger of starving. When I left home I lost weight, as though the weight were the weight of these family relationships themselves. I succumbed to the ascetic purity of that alternative religion, hunger. And now I have left home again, am in that white light again; the tree has been cut down and the light comes pouring through.

•

My daughter makes a new friend, S. She and S don't have much in common, as far as I can see. In fact, I don't like S much. She has a great collection of electronic gadgets and devices she stares at, the morbid blue light of the screen on her face. She is forever drawing my daughter aside to show her what she's looking at; the two of them stare together. Once, I go to collect my daughter from S's house and through the windows see them sitting on a large beige sofa. On the wall in front of them is a huge screen with a film playing on it. As I get closer I see that S is holding another, smaller screen in her hands: the two of them are watching that, heads together, the blue light on their faces, like incidental figures in a religious canvas, absorbed in their own corner of life while at the painting's centre Jesus is declaiming the Sermon on the Mount.

My daughter would like S to stay the night. She arrives with her overnight bag, her nail varnish collection, her gadgets. From elsewhere in the house I can hear them talking, but whenever I come in they fall silent. Over supper S replies to my questions in squeaking monosyllables. Her silence is portentous, smooth and sealed. She eats almost nothing. Later she produces packets of sweets and crisps from her overnight bag. I go in to say goodnight to them and find them lying side by side, looking at one of S's devices under the covers, the blue light of the screen on their faces. They are quiet, almost inert, but later when I go to bed I hear them murmuring and giggling. I tell them to go to sleep but as soon as I leave the murmuring starts again. Several times in the night I wake and hear it, a sound like the sound of running water or a door banging in the wind, something I know I should get up and fix but don't.

•

I go to London to meet my brother. At the sight of me his face slackens. My God, he says.

He takes me to an expensive restaurant for lunch and I eat everything on the table, eat the contents of the bread basket and the sugar lumps that come with the coffee. Afterwards he hugs me. Come and stay, he says. Bring the girls and stay for as long as you like.

•

My daughters worry that they are getting fat. They stand in front of the mirror, frowning. They prod their own flesh. It is as though some rigour has gone from our household, the rigour of the male; as though we have lost something rodlike and firm at our centre, our female bodies waxing and waning like pale moons.

A friend invites us for dinner. The children don't want to go – do we have to? they say. They seem genuinely unhappy at the prospect. When we arrive they stand right next to me; they hold on to my clothes. They seem to fear losing me in the maze of someone else's house, someone else's family. Every few minutes they yank at my sleeve. Can we go now? they say, though we've only just arrived. It strikes me that they don't like adults very much any more. When they are addressed they barely speak. Their faces are anguished.

My friend and his wife are good cooks. Theirs is a happy marriage, a joint creation of great delicacy and skill; I have always admired it, have liked to look at it and be in its presence. The food they make is expressive of themselves, healthy, moderate, and the opposite of punitive or dull. I have admired them, but things are different for me now. My admiration has become a kind of voyeurism, the broken perception of the vagabond roaming at lit windows. My children hover, tugging at my sleeve. I don't want to put people to the test: it has struck me that along with all the other losses, I might lose friendship too. I'm not equal any more with the people I know, and what is friendship but a celebration of equality?

My friend sets the table. I watch him bring out the clean plates and glasses, the gleaming cutlery. I watch him lay the places. I watch him bring out fish and bread and bowls of greenery. The kitchen is warm and comfortable. To be at this ceremony of the table again is almost painful; my daughters hover, not wanting to sit down. Can we go now? they say. My friend pulls out chairs for them, fills their plates. If you don't like it I can make you something else, he tells them. I've got other things, or maybe you just feel like eating bread. He offers the bread, and they take some. Then they eat what's in front of them, all of it. When we leave my friend gives me a loaf of his good bread. He and his wife suggest meeting again in a few days' time; they offer to take my daughters swimming with their son. My daughters don't say very much but later, when we go home, they admit that they enjoyed themselves.

•

I meet my oldest friend – J – for a drink. The children are with their father: I have begun to think that in these periods alone I ought to socialise. I see it as a kind of duty arising out of a vast and possibly terminal neglect, for I have no sense of a future: when I go out to see my friends it is in the service of an illusion. I am trying to pretend that nothing has happened, that nothing has changed, like the orchestra still playing while the *Titanic* sinks.

But it's a bad day, the day on which I meet J. Things are difficult; it's hard to talk about anything else. I can talk to J without anxiety. She knows my life and I know hers: our talk is the talk of episodes; the story itself never needs to be explained. All the same I feel guilty. The drama of my life dominates, uses up the fuel of conversation like an ugly army tank guzzling petrol. This is not equality. I'm sorry, I say, I'm sorry. I'm just so tired. I admit to J that I find it almost intolerable when the children are away. I admit that the night before I lay awake until it was light again and I could get up. I admit that I often spend these vigils in tears.

J leans across the table, grips my hand. Don't ever do that again, she says. Call me. I don't care what time of night it is, but don't ever cry on your own again. Call me instead.

•

My daughter's friendship with S has been augmented by her friendship with P. The three of them make a little giggling murmuring organism, their heads together. S's gadgets are sidelined to a degree in this more complex social structure. The blue light can't encompass three: there's always one who's out of it, who can't quite see. The entrancing properties of the screen fail to mesmerise them. It strikes me that it is like love, a trance of two that is broken by a third.

Yet the new structure of three is more boisterous, noisier, happier on the surface. I quite like P. She has some of the traits of S – crisps and nail varnish – but shares similarities with my daughter too. She is more loquacious than either of them; she chatters away, her face bright and smiling. The three of them are always together. When one goes to another's house, the third has to come along too. I am pleased for my daughter, pleased that she's found friends, though in my heart I'm disappointed. Privately I feel they're not good enough for her. Her distinct qualities, the things I know her by, don't feature much in this new social world. Who is she without those qualities? I'm not quite sure. She has taken on the interests and opinions of S and P but she doesn't seem to have rubbed off on them in quite the same way. Her old friendship with H was a relationship of greater equality, of mutual influence, of qualities shared. They were mingled together, my daughter and H, in a way that reflected well on both of them. Yet that friendship has mysteriously come to an end.

Not long after the arrival of P, another girl, D, joins the group. Now they are four, a family. D is much more to my tastes. She is observant, polite, interesting. She has a discipline about her that I like, an outward-looking beady kind of attentiveness that seems respectful of life. D does not gaze at screens. Her fingernails are unvarnished. I tell my daughter that I like her. I want to show my approval, and D has given me the opportunity.

Yes, my daughter says coolly, she's nice.

•

I ask my children what their father feeds them. Takeaways, they say. Pizza. Chicken curry from the supermarket. The tree is dead for him too, then. He was once an extravagant cook, a person who made pastry and boeuf bourguignon, who made his own mincemeat at Christmas, who made little parcels of ravioli and crimped them all around the edges. Where has it gone, that food? And where did it come from, if not from him?

I go to bed hungry and when I wake I feel a degree safer. The hunted creature, hiding, tries to make itself small. The less of me there is, the less likely it is that the arrow will find me. I cook my daughters their supper but I can't eat with them: I fear that if I do I'll forget, come out of my hiding place, expose myself to danger. I fear something terrible will happen. Increasingly, to eat seems to be to open the body: the fight-or-flight responses are disabled. It is impossible to eat and stay vigilant. Sometimes, over supper, my daughters argue and upset themselves. If I, too, were eating I might get angry with them. As it is, I spring to their aid. One Sunday evening, when I am expecting them back, the phone rings. I have made a chocolate cake for their return: it stands on a plate in the kitchen, beautifully iced. The phone call is to tell me that my daughter has had an accident at her grandparents' house, where they were staying the weekend: she is on her way to casualty, has a gash in her leg that will need stitches, so they won't be back until late. There is nothing I can do and so I stand in the kitchen, waiting. I look at the cake on its plate. It strikes me that while I was making it, my daughter was slipping on the wet path at the back of her grandparents' house and opening her knee from one side to the other on an edging stone. She returns with six stitches, and a scar that makes my heart jump into my mouth. I saw my own bone, she says. She eats a piece of cake, a small one: the shock has taken away her appetite. It's nice, she says, resting her head against my arm. Aren't you having any?

•

Days and nights of hunger, white and abstract, hunger and the feeling of excitement that is in fact its opposite, dread: I wonder whether the dying get caught up in something of this black romance, whether the courtship of death likewise feels for an instant like thrilling life. Sometimes, looking at my daughters, I remember that once I was pregnant with them, and the memory is too strange to tolerate for long. My body is far away now from that thickening, motionless state, is drifting and fading toward a blank vision of its own autonomy.

I sit and watch a war documentary with my daughters. We watch the old black-and-white footage of men coming across the Channel waters in their strange snub-nosed boats. We see them discharged on the beaches, watch them running up the sands like scuttling crabs. They are conveyed in squat trucks to a village just inland from the French coast, where the British are holding the line. The men huddle in ditches, their hands resting on the flanks of big guns all webbed in camouflage. Their faces are besmirched with mud, their tin hats strewn with leaves: they crouch like savages, grinning at the camera. The village can be seen in the near distance, a pretty place with the spire of the village church rising up through the summer trees. Back in the ditches the guns are being loaded with rounds of mortar: we watch as they fire, the men holding the kicking flanks like the thighs of a lusty woman. We watch the rounds begin to fall, puncturing the sides of buildings, shearing the tiles from the roofs, smashing street signs and windows, opening up great ragged cavities in the walls. We watch, finally, the church spire in its last moments of tranquillity: the camera lingers there on its stillness amid the treetops for what seems like an eternity, until at last the mortar strikes; and though we are expecting it, it is still shocking, still surprising to see something so blameless be destroyed. A hole is blown through its centre and its slender top bows gracefully and then topples to the earth.

•

A friend comes to visit, someone I've known for a while though not well. But lately she has come forward. She has stepped out from the background and come towards me. She brings not food but a lavender plant, a scented girlish delicate-coloured thing whose smell reminds me of childhood.

I say to her, all my memories are being taken away. Nothing belongs to me any more. I have become an exile from my own history. I say to her, I no longer have a life. It's an afterlife; it's all aftermath.

My friend has a history of her own. She too was once married; she too experienced the breaking up of that image, saw it become a pile of broken-edged pieces like the ones I carry everywhere in my hands. For a long time she lived the virginal life with her young daughter that I am living now. She was so thin you could have threaded a needle with her, had coffee flowing in her veins instead of blood, never slept because it was only when her daughter was asleep that she could live and breathe. Yet she would spend her evenings brooding and weeping instead of living. Friendship, she says, was what sustained her in that time. In Greek drama, the community shares the pain of war with the returning warriors. They come out, out into the streets to offer their love and their solicitude to those who have suffered the pain of battle. Marriage keeps other people outside, my friend says. In marriage you go away from other people, but at the end of marriage they come out to welcome you back. This is civilisation, she says. The worst thing that happened to you has brought out the best in them.

My daughters like this friend of mine. Whenever I say she's coming to visit, their faces show pleasure instead of apprehension. They don't fear her as they fear other people. When they look at her and her daughter, I suppose, they see the new reflection of themselves. Recently she got married again: my daughters and I went to her wedding and sat in the front row. My friend admits that she cried when she left the little house she shared with her daughter. She had recreated her own innocence there, washed away the bloodshed of relationship, rewound herself, spat out the fruit of the tree of knowledge. She clung, a little, to that recovered innocence; she stood at the altar for the second time in her wedding dress, trembling like a girl. I want to ask her whether it feels like real life yet, whether the feeling of aftermath can encompass even events of whose nature it is the consequence, but I don't.

•

My daughter's friend D has a birthday party. S and P, of course, are there. But when I turn up at the appointed time to collect her, it becomes clear that my daughter is the only one being sent home. S and P are staying the night at D's house: the three of them are discussing the film that has been rented for their entertainment, and that will be put on as soon as my daughter leaves.

On the way home my daughter is rigid, white, silent, but eventually she can bear it no longer and I pull the car over while she sobs against my shoulder.

Why weren't you asked to stay too? I ask her.

I don't know, she wails. I think it was D – she only wanted the others to stay, not me. They got different invitations from mine. They were talking about it all week at school.

So you knew? I said.

She nods miserably. I am so angry, with D and the parents of D, with myself, with the world for its cruelty, that I am seized by the desire to take things into my own hands. I want justice, and I want it most of all from D, because I had liked her more than the others.

Let's go back, I say. I want to talk to D's parents.

Don't, my daughter says, half-smiling though her face is still wet.

If you'd told me, I said, I would never have let you go. I would never have let that happen to you.

I suspect a calculated cruelty somewhere in my daughter's social misfortunes. It is as though she has been ostracised, cast out; as though her parents' separation is a mark of shame that has led others to spurn her. Is this civilisation too? People have come out to

comfort me, the warrior; but to her, the victim, they show a carelessness that borders on contempt.

They probably didn't even realise, she sighs, looking out of the
window into the darkness. They probably didn't even think about
it. That's just what people are like.

•

Around the corner from my house there is a florist's. I have walked
past it many times. When it is open, a green canopy is out and the
pavement beneath it is like a little scented garden filled with plants
and flowers, with containers overflowing with colour, with frothing
drifts of blooms that sway and ripple brilliantly in the grey high-
street breezes. I appreciate flowers these days. Flowers are not food.
When it is closed the canopy is retracted and the garden vanishes;
the shutters are tightly sealed across the shopfront. The facade is so
blank it is difficult even to find it amongst the other shops.

Though I am familiar with it, something about the change
from one state to the other has attracted my notice anew. I find that
I recognise its rhythms and the transformation they bring, one day
so blank and shuttered, the next so full of life. They remind me of
the way my own house now opens and closes, is either welcoming
or withdrawn, depending on the whereabouts of the children; of my
new feelings of impermanence, this gypsy life that has no past or
future, only a fragile itinerant present. The big supermarket down
the road is always open: all day its electric doors slide stolidly back
and forth, admitting and discharging streams of people. Its neon-
lit space is so impersonal and so eternal that it emanates both comfort and alienation. Inside you can forget that you're not alone, or

that you are. Sometimes I buy flowers there and put them in my daughters' bedrooms. They come in plastic sheaths, a handful of deracinated blooms, a mass-produced representation of beauty like a postcard of the *Mona Lisa*. They look pretty enough; after a few days I throw them away.

One day, walking past the florist's with a friend, we stop. The canopy is out; the pavement is in its scented glory. My friend wants to buy me some flowers. Come on, she says. Let's go in. For a moment I am frightened, as I have learned to be now of beautiful things, frightened they will contain lacerating shards of nostalgia. I don't go near the photograph album any more, don't look at the art books I once loved, don't listen to the music or read the poetry that have been my life's companions; don't walk on the hills I walked with my husband, don't contemplate foreign trips or visits to interesting places. And I don't eat, for fear that nourishment will hurt me with its inferences of pleasure. Standing outside the florist's I feel, suddenly, the completeness of my impoverishment. I feel transparent with bereavement: there is nothing, any more, I can look on and feel safe.

The plate-glass window is dark with foliage, in whose recesses the pale, waxy forms of indoor lilies and white roses stand like virginal icons. Inside there is a clean, leafy smell, and suddenly silence, tranquillity. We wander around the cool, lofty space with its fronds and ferns. At the end, behind a wooden counter, three women in green aprons are working. The counter is heaped with flowers: in their hands they hold scissors and twine. I watch for a while as they pluck the stems from the pile, deftly combining and recombining, binding the stalks with quick fingers, like classical maidens preparing their festal tributes. The bouquets grow and become splendid in their pale hands. It strikes me that they might be for a wedding, but all the same I feel a certain relief in here. There is no chromosomal presence of the male: this cool and scented place is a grove of femininity, its fecundity somehow pure, as though no conflict, no struggle of opposites needed to occur to bring these smells and shapes to completeness. I look at the different flowers in their sheaves: their pretty moulded heads, each so articulated and distinct, remind me of my daughters. I will buy some, and put them in their rooms. Perhaps I'll also buy a fern: the soft shape and something ancient about the scroll-like leaves appeals to me. Ferns are old, older than civilisation, older than man and woman, older than right and wrong. They are sexless, having neither seeds nor flowers. They are vascular plants, conductors, sensitive to contamination. They furl and unfurl, depending on the conditions. I don't know how I know these things, for I've never owned one, though I've always wanted to. I'll buy a fern, and I'll keep it alive.

At the counter the women are absorbed in their task. They haven't realised, perhaps, that we are here. We could leave and they would never know that we had come. My friend goes to the counter. Excuse me, she says, and all three of them look up.

THE RAZOR'S EDGE

My great-uncle and -aunt were husband and wife for more than
seventy years, and to talk to them was to walk the razor's edge of
marriage, where self meets other. Do you like music, uncle? Oh
yes I'm very fond of music, but *she* can't tell the difference between
Beethoven and 'Jingle Bells'. Aunt, what are your summer plans?
I'd like to go to Spain, but of course *he* won't go there, he says he
can't stand the people.

As a child I liked to visit their house, where my great-uncle's golf
clubs stood in a leather stand in the hall and my aunt's knitting machine, like a vast steel spider in its trap of yarns, could be glimpsed
through the spare-room door. Unlike ours, their Christmas-tree
decorations were the edible kind: they would give us one each when
we left, taking the little foil-wrapped chocolate shapes down from
the branches. Their sitting room smelled of Pledge and of the long,
silken-haired lapdogs they kept, and under the window was a tan-
coloured piano whose lid was always closed. My uncle often talked
of how he used to play, but one day I asked him to and stood beside him in acute embarrassment while his large old hands moved
meaninglessly around the keys. How was it possible to forget to
play the piano? It was alarming to me, at eight or ten, to learn that

competence could be lost as well as gained, that life was not merely a series of acquisitions and enlargements, of linear evolutions. Apparently it was possible to go backwards: blankness and ignorance were things to which one could be returned at any time.

He never bothered to keep it up, my aunt said.

She never liked it when I played, my uncle said.

To each other they were He and She, the primary object, the thing that was not I. They had met and married at nineteen, had children together, lived together through war and peace. As they grew older they became ever more concrete to one another, while their own selves grew increasingly formless; after seventy years of marriage they were imprisoned in one another like water imprisoned in its courses of sculpted rock. Often they would neglect to mention themselves at all, as though they had become less real to themselves, were vague spaces of pure inference, like shadows.

Are you enjoying the garden in this lovely weather, uncle?

She says that at our age we ought to be living in town because of the services.

Once, perhaps, their differences had invigorated them, but as time passed they seemed to find something more troubling in them, something whose deadliness became ever more apparent as they themselves neared death. It was as though, in old age, they were coming to the realisation that because of one another they had not lived. Then, one day, my uncle did die, and for a few weeks my aunt was as though lit up by a great flash of lightning. She blazed with wild, unrefined life, threatened to alter the will that represented her first experience of financial independence, played one family member off against another, bristled with new opinions and a new intransigence that could, earlier in her life, have become authority but now was a tragicomic parody of it. She uttered heresies on the subjects of marriage and motherhood that had the gunpowder smell of personal truths, argued with and disinherited her children, and then, all at once, like the sea after a storm, retracted into a profound passivity. She lay in bed, beside a small framed photograph of my uncle taken in earlier years. 'That's him' was all she'd say, to those who visited and who, abruptly, she no longer appeared to recognise. She was moved to a nursing home, and in the beige hush of her featureless room lay day in and day out with the photograph in her hand, unspeaking and unmoving, until she herself was no more.

•

I have entered a phase of resistance, of reaction. The sight of families makes me irritable. In the park they pass me on bicycles, mother and father and children, all clad in safety helmets and luminescent strips and rucksacks containing emergency supplies. They make manifest their own fear: their obsession with their safety is evident. Of what, precisely, are they afraid? They call out orders and directions to one another, as though the rest of us were uncomprehending natives.

I blame Christianity – as far as I can see, that's where the trouble started. The holy family, that pious unit that sucked the world's attention dry while chastising it for its selfishness, that drew forth its violence and then in an orgy of self-glorification consigned it to eternal shame, that sentenced civilisation to two millennia of institutionalised dishonesty; compared with the households of Argos and Thebes, that family has a lot to answer for. In the park I view them through narrowed eyes, these well-organised heirs of Christian piety. They seem to me to have taken all the fun out of life: spoilsports! What happened to passionate conflict and reunion, the kinetic of man and woman that drives the life blood around the body? These men and women now wear protective helmets to pass through a public park. From a bench I ruminate on it darkly. The day feeble Joseph agreed to marry pregnant Mary the old passionate template was destroyed. That was an act of fundamental dishonesty all round: the new template of marriage – a lie! The family was reinvented, a cult of sentimentality and surfaces; became an image, bent on veiling reality – the stable in all its faux-humility, the angels and the oxen, the manger to which kings come on bended knee, the 'parents' gathered adoringly round the baby – an image of child-worship, of sainted unambivalent motherhood, of gutless masculinity and fatherly impotence. And it still comes through the twenty-first-century letterbox at Christmastime; I remind myself not to send any cards this year.

These days, of course, the ancient Greeks are back in fashion: we find their honesty, their emotional violence, their flouting of taboos therapeutic and refreshing. We sit in exquisitely neutral consulting rooms, discuss our Electra complex; but at the end of it all we go home to the manger and the holy child, to the roles and relationships that constitute our deepest sense of family reality, though they themselves are not real. Reality is our visceral knowledge and desires: the image exists to control them, and out of them creates a strange half-reality of its own. And I too was once in uneasy thrall to that image, directed by it as by a puppeteer unseen in the darkness of the wings. Its propriety and its safety chastised me, consigned me to eternal shame; yet it seemed the only thing it had to teach – like any image – was to be more like itself.

So now I find that the sight of those cycling families calls for the intellectual equivalent of a stiff drink, and I procure it in the form of the ancient dramas. There are no devoted mothers here, no perfect children, no protective dutiful fathers, no public morality. There is only emotion, and the attempt to tame it, to shape it into a force for good. The question of what constitutes authority, in the tempestuous Greek world of feeling and psychological fate, with its mingling of mortality and divinity, is eternal and unresolved. It is a question with which I am preoccupied too: what will authority be, where will it come from, in my post-familial household?

•

There's a moment in Sophocles's play *Antigone* when something new is born, or rather, when one thing becomes two; when one kind of authority is no longer enough and must produce a second, just as Christianity would itself propose two authorities, the authority of the creator – God – and the authority – Jesus – of self-sacrifice. The play is set in Thebes, in the immediate wake of the Oedipal drama. King Oedipus has blinded himself and been expelled to wander the catacombs of Athens as a beggar. His wife Jocasta, having learned that she was also his mother, has killed herself. His two sons, Eteocles and Polylectes, have murdered one another in their failed attempt to share power. Creon is Jocasta's brother: Oedipus's sons being dead, the burden of leadership has passed to him.

I feel a certain sympathy for Oedipus. His story expresses what to me seems the central human tragedy, the fact that we lack knowledge of the very things that drive us to our fate. We do not fully know what it is that we do, and why. Oedipus did not know that his wife was also his mother. He did not know that the rude stranger he killed at the crossroads was his father. Yet he was punished for these acts as though they had been conscious. There were people – Oedipus's adoptive parents, for instance – who did know something of his origins but did not disclose it. It is a kind of authority, this hidden knowledge. Sometimes, when my children have done something wrong, I pretend that I don't know it; I wait to see whether they will find their own path to contrition, their own way to make amends. But what if they don't? I have to tell them that I know, that I saw, and in doing so somehow the truth passes from me to them. My authority is no longer truthful; the truth becomes the truth of their own acts.

In *Oedipus Rex* every kind of authority is damaged by precisely this process. Leadership and masculinity, the concept of family, marriage itself: all has become a perversion, the sibling bond turned murderous, motherhood mutated into self-destruction. The world Creon has inherited is a post-authority, post-familial world: it is aftermath, and Creon has the job of governing it. But how do you make people obey you, respect you, believe in you and in the new reality you represent? Creon's idea is that you give commands and then don't turn back on them, no matter what – a strategy the modern parent, presiding over chaos and unrule, occasionally adopts, only to find themselves insisting on a course of action long after its necessity and even its rationality have passed. This is more or less Creon's fate. The body of Polylectes, Oedipus's son, is still lying where it fell at the city limits. Creon decides he needs to send out a strong message of disapproval of the Oedipal household, in order to mark his separation from it. He proclaims that Polylectes will not be buried, but instead must lie there to rot, picked at by ravens and wild animals. No one is allowed to touch the body. The punishment for doing so will be death.

Antigone is Polylectes's sister, daughter of Oedipus and Jocasta. She inhabits an aftermath of her own: hers has been the experience of intimate loss. Her family has been atomised; questions of identity, of moral choice, that might once have been family matters have devolved to her. She has been awoken and forced into active being. She has become herself, yet this self has been contaminated by the drama of her parents. Therefore she is only as good as what she does, as what she chooses to do. And what she chooses to do is bury Polylectes, because having thought about Creon's edict she can find no justice or logic in it. She challenges his authority with an emotional authority of her own that has stronger links with justice, with truth. Creon asks, astonished, whether she realises the punishment for her act will be death. Isn't she afraid to die? No, she replies, she isn't afraid of death. What she's afraid of is neglecting to do something that she knows to be right. Doesn't she realise she's breaking the law? he says. It was only you who made that law, she replies. Why should I obey it?

'Now she would be the man, not I, if she defeated me and did not pay for it,' Creon says to himself. 'Though she [is] my niece, or closer still than all [my] family, she shall not escape the direst penalty.' And so Creon manoeuvres himself into a position where his authority will directly attack and destroy what he himself loves and values the most, in order to nourish and sustain itself. He summons Teiresias the seer for reassurance. Creon believes Teiresias to be wise, prizes his advice, as one prizes the advice of certain friends until they say what you don't want to hear. And Teiresias, indeed, gives him the darkest warnings: 'Once more you tread the razor's

edge,' he says. What he means is that Creon's authority is recreating the very perversity from which it was born. It has become the
form that imprisons truth and must be broken. Creon falls out with
Teiresias and insults him in every possible way, but afterwards he is
more honest with himself. This, after all, is aftermath, the second
harvest: life with knowledge of what has gone before. He admits
that he is frightened. He admits that what frightens him most is
the idea that he will have to sacrifice himself in the name of authority, that true responsibility is an act of self-destruction.

'To yield is very hard,' he says. 'But to resist and meet disaster,
that is harder still.'

•

In the school holidays I take my children horse riding in Devon.
Their desire to ride horses is so consistent it almost seems impersonal. It seems to be something I can bank on.

I rent somewhere to stay near a riding school where they will
ride every day. I drive west, through unfamiliar hills. I am shaking with nerves; in fact, I can't remember what it feels like to be
at ease. This ceaseless effort to manufacture normality is a kind of
forger's art, so laborious compared with the facility that created
the original. It is a fine evening and the sun slants long and golden
from the horizon. For me these voyages are like the first outings of
the Vikings into the mystery of the ocean, by turns terrifying and
thrilling: I have no idea what will happen, what we will find. It
is the idea that we won't find anything at all that terrifies me. Yet
what exactly we are looking for I don't know.

At a service station we stop, and stand in the car park drinking hot chocolate with the sharp western sunset in our eyes. The place we are going is a picturesque country town near Dartmoor: everyone seems to agree it's lovely there, though I'm not sure anyone I spoke to had actually been. Like tales of America, these were the rumours that drew us from the safety of home. But I feel buoyed up all the same, by the obliging beauty of the landscape and by the feeling – so powerful and so fleeting, so hard to understand or defend – that we have been liberated from the strictures of some authority and are free. I don't identify this authority as my husband: the authority is marriage itself, and in these moments of liberty I feel him to be just as browbeaten by it as me, feel, almost, that I could conscript him into my own escape and reencounter him there, in non-marriage, both of us free.

It is dark by the time we get to the town. The place is deserted: at the house the owner has left us a scribbled note and a key. We stand on the long, sloping cobbled street with our bags. Through the darkness comes the sound and smell of water. A broad river is just below us: it turns like a dark snake in its courses; its black surface gleams. The town is a soundless heaped outline in the night, of roofs and spires and well-kept streets. Its beauty and its desertion are unnerving. It is as though some disaster has just occurred here and all the people have run away.

Inside, the house is a dank-smelling labyrinth of corridors and fire doors. There is torn carpet underfoot and heaps of junk and old furniture piled against the walls. Instantly I know that it has found me out, chaos, malevolent disorder: for the past few months it has shadowed me and I have fended it off, day and night, and now it seems I have opened the door to it. The thing is, I believe in chaos now: it's normality I've lost faith in. It transpires that we have not rented the whole house but only a section of it: the note directs us upstairs, up steep tenebrous staircases boxed in by irregular partition walls to a door at the top. We let ourselves into a dark flat. The electric lights reveal a crush of brown furniture, some beds with padded floral headboards, some gilt-framed posters of rural scenes. I decide that I've over-reacted. I decide there's nothing actually intolerable here.

It's quite nice really, I say to the children, as though we make a habit of staying in places such as this, and can compare them to one another. In fact they have had the good fortune never to have been somewhere like it before. But I'm not interested in teaching them a lesson.

Yes, they repeat, standing in the doorway with their coats on, it's quite nice really.

And tomorrow you're going riding, I say.

They fall silent. They're not sure they want to go riding after all. They're not sure they feel like it.

I make them supper on the two-ring electric burner in the kitchenette. I tuck them up beneath the floral headboards. I sympathise, I console, I sit at their bedsides until far into the night, but in the morning I drive them to the riding school and I leave them there.

•

At mid-morning there is a great commotion out in the hall, loud voices and banging and then a thumping sound that gets louder and louder until I realise it's coming up the stairs. There is a pause, the sound of noisy breathing on the landing; the door to the flat flies open and a woman barges into the cramped hall.

Oh hello, she says at the sight of me sitting at the table. I didn't realise you were in here.

I take this to be the owner of the building. She is so dishevelled it is hard to get a sense of her. Vaguely I apprehend a large mounded body, a shock of grey frizzy hair, a clutch of big yellow teeth, a red leathery face grotesquely made up. The teeth are bared: she is either panting or smiling, I can't tell. She has a pair of crutches strapped to her arms on which she leans forward and with which she occasionally gestures, like the forelegs of some gigantic insect.

It's a long way up, she pants, but I make a point of doing it, no matter what they say. You can't let things get out of bounds, can you? It happens without you noticing, then all at once you find you're bedridden.

Looking at her, I'm surprised she did manage to get up the stairs, for she has only one leg. I ask her if she would like to sit down.

Are you all right? she says sharply in response. Her voice is rather loud and braying; I notice her clothes, rainbow-coloured draperies in chiffon and velvet. Like it here? Such a lovely house, isn't it? These are our best rooms. Her glance darts around. What's that you're doing? she says, looking at what's on the table.

Writing, I say.

I'm a writer too, she says, leering delightedly at me. What a coincidence!

Yes, it is, I say.

Of course, I don't write under my own name, she adds, significantly.

There is a pause.

Are you all right? she says again. It's nice up here, isn't it? Perfect for writing. Really I should come up here and do some writing myself, only I'm so madly busy all the time. She gives me a hostessy kind of twinkle. Then she says:

But I'm afraid I'm going to have to move you.

Move me? I say.

It's only downstairs, she says. It's just that some other people want to be up here. They want to rent it long-term. They're a family, she says. Lovely people. They're relocating to this area and they absolutely have to have it.

I tell her that she should have told me this in advance.

Oh, but you see I didn't know! she cries. They only called last night, and they're desperate, poor things. The girl is absolutely at her wits' end – they've just come back from Geneva I think it is, where her husband's some big cheese, and she's had to make all the arrangements herself, and my heart just bled for her really. The thing is, she's got the children to think of. Such a sweet family, she says.

I ask her when she expects us to move.

Well, she says, if you don't mind, then right away would be best. They're coming tonight and the cleaner needs to get in – you'll be absolutely fine downstairs. You're really tucked away down there, she says. Perfect for writing!

'Downstairs', it turns out, is the basement, a big windowless room crammed with furniture, whose ceiling is so low the hairs on the top of my head brush it as I walk. It takes me three or four journeys up and down the stairs to bring down the suitcases we had just unpacked. I pass numerous people on the staircase, in the hall. It is eleven o'clock in the morning, but in the basement you wouldn't know whether it was night or day. I stand in the electric light from the overhead bulb, the suitcases at my feet. I can hear the thump of the woman descending the cellar stairs. She puts her head around the door.

Everything all right? she says, panting. Got to run now – so much to do! You've got one or two people above you, Poles, lovely family, they're usually very quiet. Oh and by the way, the men are here today doing some building work in the hall, but hopefully the noise won't disturb you too much. Bye bye!

And with a wink of her fronded eye, she is gone.

•

I go for a walk. I have to: I can't stay in the basement for even a few minutes. The clear skies of the night before have been succeeded by blustering wind and cloud. It starts to rain. I think of the children riding their horses in the bad weather. I can't find a path out of the town into the countryside and I end up walking along busy roads, and then through a kind of forest where broad sandy tracks pass amid shaved stretches of felled trees, and lorries piled with pale logs trundle to and fro.

When I return I call the witch, as I now think of her. It takes time to track her down: I have to try several different numbers.

Oh it's you, she says.

I tell her she needs to find us somewhere else to stay, immediately. I tell her I wouldn't keep a dog in that basement. I tell her her conduct has been fraudulent. She needs to rectify the situation by the time my children return from the riding school.

While I'm speaking she makes little exclamations, 'yes' and 'oh' and 'oh dear' and 'of course'. The more she whimpers, the more

brutal I am. I enjoy it: this must be what it feels like to beat someone up. Yet I think about her missing leg and feel afraid.

She says that we can come and stay in her very own house, a
lovely place out in the countryside. She'd like us to; she'd like to
make amends. I don't trust her: I say I want to see it first. She offers
to drive me out there in her car to look. I sit on a suitcase in the
basement and wait. The building is full of the sounds of drilling.
There are footsteps going to and fro across the ceiling, voices, the
noise of a television on loud. The witch arrives, clad in a miscellany
of crushed velvet draperies of purple and cerise; I follow her out to
her car and get in. The car is filthy. She has a special arrangement of
gears and levers for driving. On the journey she talks. I don't listen.
I am silent, except to ask her how far it is. Oh, not very far, she says.
It's really very close. Just a few miles.

We pass over the snaking river and out of the picture-postcard
town, out into unfamiliar countryside. I sit and stare out of the
window. In the rain the patchwork of fields and buildings looks
desolate. At a petrol station she stops, and I stare out of the window
as she hobbles around the pump, the crushed velvet lurid in the
drizzle. She goes inside. I watch her talking to the girl behind the
till, watch her mouth moving, watch her throwing her head back to
laugh. She talks for a long time. Eventually she returns. We drive
for half an hour, forty-five minutes. I ask her when we will be there.
Oh, any minute now, she says. It's just around the corner.

Finally, as we are driving along a section of dual carriageway
through low hills, she veers unexpectedly off the road and draws to
a halt outside a house, so abruptly that we are thrown forward in
our seats. We have pulled up at a cottage with crooked chimney-
pots. There are pieces of broken furniture in the front garden, and

rags hanging at the tiny windowpanes. The road lies so close to the front gate that the passing traffic makes it swing on its hinges. We get out of the car.

I need to get back soon for my children, I say.

Oh don't worry, she says. There'll be plenty of time for that.

We go in through the gate, through the front garden. The witch jerks open the front door.

Welcome to my humble abode, she says.

She leads me through dark dusty rooms filled with furniture, her crutches thumping across the floorboards; along crooked low-ceilinged corridors, up a creaking staircase with a cobwebbed window at the top. I look out of it, down on to a concrete yard where a big mangy Alsatian is tied by a chain. We pass a cluttered room with a wheelchair in it and a mechanical hospital bed, unmade. There is a man on the landing, holding a little girl in ponytails by the hand. He smiles, says something in a language I don't recognise. We pass through a low doorway, into a small room with a narrow single bed, whose tiny window looks out on to the dual carriageway. On the floor there are empty wine bottles. The room is cold and smells of rot. There are bits of dirty newspaper tacked to the walls.

Well, nothing will disturb you in *here*, she says. Enjoy your writing!

And with that she limps out and closes the door.

I sit on the edge of the bed, my hands in my lap. An hour passes, perhaps more. Then I hear the sound of a car pulling up outside. I go to the window and look. A woman comes through the front gate and up the path. She is very fat. She wears tight clothes, a short skirt, a spangled top with a plunging neckline. Her plump neck is roped in jewellery. Her synthetic black hair is piled up on

her head. She waddles to the front door and knocks. Below me the
door opens. I hear the two women conversing. There is what sounds
like an exchange of obscenities, then cackling laughter. Presently I
see the two of them going off together down the path. The witch
has dressed herself up too: she wears a tight carmine-coloured dress
in which her misshapen body takes on a mournful kind of beauty.
They get in the other woman's car, a tiny battered hatchback into
which it seems the two of them can't possibly fit, and they roar
away, a plume of black smoke at the exhaust.

•

Much later, when I am back at home and the children have returned to school, I find a novel in a second-hand bookshop. It has
a bright red cover with silver writing on. It is garish, splashy – I
turn it over in my hands. The novel is self-published; I vaguely recognise the name on the cover, and standing there read a chapter or
two. Their subject is a woman's loss of value as she ages, the decay
of the body that was once the source of her human authority, her
feelings of rage at being left alone, men and children having gone
away. She shocks people with her desire to live: they expect her to
give in, to go quietly, to hide herself away somewhere and politely
rot. And so she has come to enjoy their shock, their disapproval. She
dresses herself in garish colours. She goes out, out to skirmish with
the world, and whether or not she is wounded on that battlefield,
whether she is brought down and beaten and meets her end, that
end is better than the end society has in mind for her, is a suicidal
kind of rebellion, an attempt to go out in a blaze of glory.

I talk to my friends sometimes about my imprisonment in the

witch's house. What did you do? people say. How did you get away?
What happened to the children? I don't tell them – not quite – how
difficult I found it to leave, how I stayed there while dusk fell over
the hills and the rooms darkened; how I felt that this was something I ought to make right, the ugliness and disorder of this place.
I felt I ought to love it, for all at once I understood that its failure
came not from some evil intention but from the fact that it was
unloved. That failure had frightened me, menaced me, more than
the most direct threat to my safety would have; I wanted to protect
myself from it, protect my children, but sitting alone in that house,
I felt that the true achievement, the true safety, the true authority
might lie beyond the instinct to safeguard what was mine.

I called a taxi. I wrote a note saying I was sorry and left it on
the table. I called the riding school and explained. Then I waited
there, in the dusk, until the taxi's headlights swept like search-
beams across the front windows as it came off the road to find me.

X Y Z

Every week I drive for forty-five minutes along the coast to see Y. I go in the morning, when my children are at school. The journey out of the city is fast at first, then slow once the road passes out into the countryside and narrows to a single lane, where the traffic constantly crawls without stopping or ceasing, a turgid metal river creeping through deserted green banks.

Y lives in a suburban cul-de-sac on the outskirts of a town that I never see, for I reach his house first and have no reason to go any further. I have been instructed not to park in the cul-de-sac itself: I have to leave my car on the road at the bottom and walk up. The black tarmacked surface winds among houses and many trees; except for the noise the wind makes in the foliage it is always silent there, and rarely do I pass another living being on the road, though sometimes I glimpse dim forms through windows set back behind lawns, on whose glass the green canopy of trees makes rippling primordial patterns of shadow and light. At the entrance to Y's property there is an apple tree. The first time I saw it there was blossom bursting from the branches. The explosive white startled me, frothing out so wildly and yet staying so still, like a white wave frozen in the moment of its breaking. Beyond it are the gates to his driveway. His house has two entrances, one at the front and one at the side, and it is at the side door that on my visits I ring the bell, and stand listening to the wind soughing in the branches, and wait.

•

At a party in London I meet Z.

A room that is too warm and full of people, with plush fitted carpet underfoot in which we all seem somehow mired. There are waiters circulating with trays of canapés. There is a viscosity in the atmosphere, a thickness in which everything becomes slowed. I watch people's faces, watch their mouths moving. I seem to hear everything and nothing. Though it is evening the sun comes hot through the city windows. I had to walk around the park across the road for an hour before I could bring myself to go in. I don't want to talk; I have nothing to say.

Z is a man. What am I to a man, and what is he to me? I haven't thought about it: I don't go out very often. I feel like a soldier come back from a war, full of experiences that have silenced me. I cannot return to innocence, the innocence of the first encounter of female and male. It becomes clear that Z is a veteran too; he too is full of the swarming silence of experience. But we have fought in different wars.

I don't know him. We talk about cities, about Bangkok and Los Angeles and Moscow. We are strangers and this conversation is a kind of rocket, fast-moving and airborne, keeping us up above the surface of things. It is as though we are orbiting the earth from a great distance and observing its landmarks, its populous centres. There is a freedom to it that at any moment could become terror. Every few minutes a waiter comes past and stops with a tray. After a while I become familiar with these rotating offerings, can begin to anticipate their sequence and character. I begin to know the tray of celery sticks standing in a glossy mound of mayonnaise, the tray of little pastry cups with something yellow and sticky inside, the tray of shiny brown cocktail sausages: when they come round I notice that the mayonnaise has formed a kind of crust, that the pastry cups have become so steeped in rejection that it is impossible to do anything but reject them again. I begin to anchor myself in this familiarity as a weed anchors itself in the merest thimbleful of soil, but then, when the waiter appears at the expected moment with his tray of cocktail sausages, Z waves him irritably away. He has had enough of these interruptions. A feeling of anxiety grips me. The waiter retreats. I feel, somehow, bereft. I feel that nothing might ever come my way again, that I am destitute, like a child lost in a hectic foreign city, in Los Angeles, in downtown Bangkok. As the waiter passes me I put out my hand and snatch a sausage from the tray and I put it in my mouth.

•

X calls. Our conversation is like chewing on barbed wire, like eating ground glass. Our talk is a well that has been poisoned, but all the same I drink from it.

•

In Y's room I sit in the armchair. It is a stiff old-womanish chair, though like everything else in Y's room it feels solid and clean and as if it doesn't quite belong to anybody. Y sits in a beige leather swivel chair with a sparkling steel skeleton and a deep padded seat. He is tall and what used to be called rangy. He has a beard, grey. I see him as an assemblage of joints and rods, like a large mathematical instrument; his big straight limbs pivot in their sockets with a mechanical ease and alignment in the clear morning light of his room. He is dressed in the manner of a Christian missionary or an aid worker, in clothes whose insignificance almost constitutes a significance of its own. Other than in this room his maleness has no context for me, and so like the chair he sits in he appears to be made of steel. I don't mind it. I am broken, and steel might repair me.

I say, I don't ever want you to tell me that I think too much. If you say that I'll leave.

Y is silent for a long time. When he begins to speak, it is to outline for me the codes of conduct pertaining to his consulting room. He talks about timescales, the longer view, the inflexibility of the fifty minutes that is both its weakness and its strength. He goes on to discuss the general import of our relationship, the symbolism of its contractual essence, its politics of transference, seduction and blame. I begin to feel like a horse struggling while a harness is put over its head. He refers to himself in all this rather frequently, as though he were an established landmark in my life, and I feel a spasm of vulnerability on his behalf. He is like a priest who has forgotten to check that his congregation believes in God before he sermonises them. Y's religion is psychoanalysis, and I have not come to worship: I need to be converted first.

I say, I'm not sure this will work. I'm not sure this will do any good.

I feel jealous of Y's beliefs. They seem to take up all his attention. I want to attack them, to damage them. I want to humiliate them by not believing in them myself.

Y looks slightly startled, but only like an actor would. He cocks his head to one side. Then tell me why you're here, he says.

It is strange to discuss my marriage in this room; its neutrality is almost chastising, makes the story both more lurid and more sombre, like the orderly courtrooms in which suited committees analyse war crimes, carefully dissect individual acts of thoughtless brutality and havoc over matching coffee cups. It is aftermath, the thing that happens once reality has occurred. Will I ever find reality again, bloodied and pulsing, find my way out of this room and back down the road along which I came? Y listens, stroking his large knuckles. I talk and talk, as though I am on the stand. I talk in expectation of a judgement, for or against me I do not know. Finally he opens his mouth to speak.

We have to stop now, he says.

·

Z comes to see me. We take a walk in the countryside. I expected him to bring something – I don't really know what – but he comes empty-handed. He is quiet, nervous, taller than I remembered. He seems different every time I look at him. His face and form change by the minute. I don't know him. If he had brought something at least I'd know that. But he seems not to want to make himself manifest. He is mysterious.

As we walk we talk. In our conversation I keep missing my footing. It is as though I'm expecting there to be a step down and there isn't one. I'm used to talking to someone else. Z walks quickly;

I have to run to keep up. He says, narrative is the aftermath of violent events. It is a means of reconciling yourself with the past. He says, the violence in the *Odyssey* is a story told afterwards, in a cave.

I want to live, I say. I don't want to tell my story. I want to live.

Z says, the old story has to end before a new one can begin.

We are in a downland valley, where warm tousling winds roll across meadows of long grass and wildflowers. A silver river runs through it in slow skating curves to the sea. It is quiet here, but there is a clamour in my head. I feel charged with tension, as the sky is charged with electricity before a storm; I feel the approach of some great disturbance. The mechanism of life is jammed, the way minutes and hours and days knit themselves, gather in the separate strands and knit them fast together into life, into being – it is jammed, blocked, broken. The clamour is like a maniacal orchestra, crashing and clanging its gongs and cymbals. I can't process what I see or hear or feel: impressions, sensations pour in but they can't get out again; they mount and mount in the silent valley until I feel that I will burst with them.

Z and I drive without speaking back to the city.

•

That night I call X. I don't know why I call him. I just want to talk, like a climber trapped in a snowstorm on a mountaintop calling home. It is rescue she hopes for, but perhaps she is stranded too far and too high to be rescued. Perhaps she just wants to say goodbye. The roaming itch that drove her away from home, away from ordinary satisfactions, away from the life at sea level, remains mysterious even as it devours her in that cold and lonely place. She calls what she left, calls home.

X answers. Our conversation is like chewing on razor blades, like eating caustic soda. Our talk is a well that has been poisoned, but all the same I drink from it.

•

I say to Y, marriage is a mode of manifestation. It absorbs disorder and manifests it as order. It takes different things and turns them into one thing. It receives chaos, diversity, confusion, and it turns them into form.

Y strokes his knuckles.

I say, marriage is civilisation and now the barbarians are cavorting in the ruins.

Yet we find ruins exquisite, Y says.

He seems to be accusing me of sentimentalising. He seems to suspect me of nostalgia.

People overthrow their governments and then they want them back, I say. They evict their dictator and then they don't know what to do with themselves. They complain that everything is chaos now, that there is no law and order any more.

Y raises his eyebrows at the word 'dictator'.

I tell him about the walk with Z. If I was looking for a new dictator, Z didn't get the job. I tell him of the way I showed him around my house, bought flowers, made him a beautiful lunch, like a small country advertising itself for invasion. I tell him of the valley I took him to, the loveliest place for miles around with its band of silver running through it, the way I showed it to him as proudly as if I'd made it myself.

Yet the mechanism had jammed, the very knit and weave of life knotted into madness.

Is it male attention I want, or male authority?

Is there a difference? Y says, rummaging pleasurably in his beard.

Z attended to my vision but he wouldn't take possession of it. He backed away and was silent; it remained my house, my valley.

•

X talks. X is a talker. He is like a well signposted museum: it's easy to find your way around, to see what he chooses to display. There are new things there now, new people, new opinions, new tastes in evidence; the old ones have been taken down to the archive, I suppose, shut away in darkness, left to the mercy of rot and floods.

But he doesn't like me to visit, doesn't want to talk to me any more. The museum guards follow me closely; perhaps they suspect I'm going to steal or deface something. I keep enquiring after what is no longer part of the collection. X furrows his brow, as though he has difficulty recollecting it, this past to which I insist on referring. As soon as he can, he shows me out. The big institutional door, so handsome and polished, so reassuringly heavy, closes in my face.

•

Z comes to the house with a bag of tools. He fixes the broken shower, the rusty bicycles, the pipe that leaks water into the kitchen wall.

Are all these pieces of paper bills? he says.

I don't know, I say. I don't want to open them. I want to live.

Z opens one and reads it. He raises his eyebrows, gives a small smile.

It's a speeding fine, he says.

•

There is at first a feeling of deceleration, of a panicky loss of power, as though the fuel tank has run dry. I feel as if I've broken down in the middle of nowhere. It's so quiet here, and so unfamiliar. I don't know where I am. I hear a whisper, see a gleam of light, a faint ripple on the surface of water. The silver river moves quietly in its courses; the bulrushes stir and shift, the meadow dissolves in the blur of advancing dusk. Darkness is coming, night, and I am far from home. In the distance the sea is soft and calm. It glimmers and grows pale as the day leaves it. The blue dusk deepens; the darkness falls. Along the shore there are other places, houses and towns, but only when the darkness comes can I see them. Distant lights, mounded like embers in the blackness, and they are there and I am here.

The tree at Y's front gates has apples on it. They are as startlingly abundant as the white blossom was, yet they are round and hard and heavy, the pregnancy after the white bridal whirl of romance. Y wants to know where my cruelty comes from and why I am so wedded to it. Cruelty is an aspect of civilisation, I say. Cruelty is part of power; it's like the army; you bring it out when you need to. But all your cruelty is against yourself, he says. I laugh. He is displeased. Why do you laugh? he says sharply. I tell him I don't have much time for the doctrine of self-love. I see it as a kind of windless primordial swamp, and I don't want to be stuck there. What he calls cruelty I call the discipline of self-criticism. A woman who loves herself is unprotected. She will be invaded, put in chains, left there in the primordial swamp to love her heart out.

Y looks at his watch. We need to stop now, he says.

•

I go with Z to the cinema and when we come out I say something about the film that he doesn't understand. I say it again, then I say it in a different way, but he still can't see it, can't grasp my meaning. I feel, suddenly, that I've lost my power of communication. The loss feels as tangible as if I'd boarded an aeroplane and flown to a country whose people didn't speak my language, nor I theirs.

Z lives alone. His flat is simple and of modest size. In my own house I am never still; I charge from top floor to bottom and back again, from room to room, like a dynamo revolved and revolved by some elemental feeling of dread. I'm trying to keep the house alive. I worry that if I stop I'll forget, that I'll look up again to find that it has become a ruin. Sometimes it feels as though I inhabit a mirage, a projection; that the real house has gone but the children don't know, don't realise that I'm behind the curtain like the Wizard of Oz, frantically turning knobs and adjusting microphones to keep the illusion going. In Z's flat I don't move. I can't: there's nowhere to go. I watch the light moving and changing through the rooms. I listen to the dim sounds from outside. I become aware of myself, too close, like a stranger sitting down right next to me in a train carriage full of empty seats.

Z waits for the cloud of the cinema trip to pass over, waits for the clamour to die down. He cooks, runs a bath, gives me a book to read. He is as sensitive to events as the bulrushes are to the stroking wind. His flat is quiet. Nothing ever changes there: when I visit, I find everything exactly where it was the time before. He says, sometimes you say things before you've understood them yourself. For you the saying is a kind of working out, he says, like doing a sum on a bit of paper. You can't always expect people to grasp it. But I want you to know what I mean, I say. So do I, he says. I want to know what you mean.

It's late at night, too late to run away from something whose nature I can't in any case discern. It's just a shape in the darkness, understanding or its opposite, I can't tell.

●

Y says that my relationship with him – Y – is helpful because it can't ever become sexual. He claims that I find this relieving. He says this is why, with him, I feel safe.

I talk a lot with Y about X but increasingly I find I am reluctant to mention Z. In the neutrality of Y's consulting room the whole bloodstained past has been unravelled, the war with X, its causes and key battles, its moments of drama and shame, but of Z very little is said. I find that I am protective of the silence around Z. The old war can be turned into words, but a living silence ought not to be disturbed. Things might be growing there, like seeds under newly ploughed earth. Week after week Y and I sit like Odysseus in his cave, processing the violent past in reams of talk. The present is a talking present; but of the future what can be said?

The apple tree outside has shed its leaves. It has started to rain, after the long dry clanging days of summer. The drive to

Y's house is slow, the windows wet with condensation, the lorries sending up sprays of muddy water, the sky overhead sagging with iron-grey clouds. When I walk up the cul-de-sac the wind buffets and whirls among the trees and houses. Sometimes I wonder why I come here when the coming is so iterative, so forced. Having to come here sometimes feels like the biggest problem I have. I feel like a lonely man visiting a brothel, the money changing hands, paying for understanding as some people pay for love. And just as that is not love, so this cannot be understanding. What, then, is it?

I am certain Y will say that my feelings of rebellion against psychoanalysis are predictable and meaningful; that my rebellion can be encompassed by that against which I am rebelling. Occasionally we have discussed the ways in which a therapy might be brought to an end, but it always sounds to me rather like dying, long and drawn-out, a matter not of choice but of some greater law of genesis and cessation of which we are, apparently, at the mercy.

I don't say these things aloud: perhaps unwittingly, Y has alluded from his web of talk to the existence of the nonverbal universe, and I intend to go and live there.

•

Love, Z says. Do you want to use that word?

Make me something, I say. Give me something. Bring me something. Not love, or at least, not only love.

Z sighs, shakes his head, reminds me to pay my speeding fine. I lean against him. His skin is always so hot. When I get close enough, it feels like sitting next to a fire. Yet when I am further away he is a purely reflective surface, like the sea in certain moods. I watch him, watch the light move across him, watch the rippling surface. The clocks go back; the days get darker, but the sea retains its light. I buy a coat, because it's winter now.

TRAINS

In the town she came from it always felt like there were more people in the cemeteries than walking around the place on their own legs. The cemeteries were bigger than the parks in that town. High-speed trains crossed the flat countryside nearby in great bounds, Paris to Antwerp, Zurich to Brussels, but she never felt the trains contained living people either. They passed behind the lines of headstones, a blur of velocity, moving so fast it almost looked like they too were standing still.

But then one day she got on a train herself, and now it was the town that seemed to move. She sat next to her suitcase and stared out of the carriage window as it all moved away from her, the grey houses and rain-darkened streets, the concrete factory yards, the cemetery under the same low furrowed sky; moved away from her like a stranger who has passed her on the pavement and walked on, without recognition or regret.

•

She is scared. She thought in the new place she would feel free but she doesn't. She feels tied by long tethers. When she makes the slightest movement, she feels it all along the length of her bonds.

The man collected her from the station. Welcome to England, he said, and then his talk ran away from her like a cataract going over a cliff. He wore young people's clothes, a leather jacket, red sneakers on his feet. On the car journey she understood almost nothing of what he said. She sat rigid, frozen beside him. It was as if the car was full of noise, the sound of mad crashing and banging and shrieking, but he couldn't hear it. She sat in her seat, frozen, glancing at him sometimes while he talked.

Out of the window she saw tilting streets of white houses, every street crowded with parked cars, and big birds picking at litter on the pavements. When she got out of the car she looked up. The sky was much further away than it was at home, and full of chasing clouds. She followed the man up the steps to the front door of a house and waited while he searched his pockets for his keys. The woman was standing in the hall. Sonia couldn't see what she looked like because she instantly came forward, startling her, and kissed her on both cheeks. She took Sonia's bag, the little handbag with the chain of square gold links, and put it on the hall table. She asked questions, tea, did Sonia want a cup of tea, and Sonia shook her head. Then she turned and went up the stairs, still talking. Sonia followed her. She opened the door to a room with a bed in it, a wardrobe, a desk, and Sonia went in. Then she said something and closed the door and went away.

Sonia stood there in her coat. She needed her handbag but it was downstairs. She wanted a cigarette. She went to the window and looked down. There was a little garden, flowers, a tree. There was a knock at the door and the man came in with her suitcase. He put it down beside the bed and went away again. She stood in her coat and waited.

•

'How is it?' Kurt said on the phone. 'What's it like? How is the house?'

'Big,' she said.

'Did you give them their gifts?'

Kurt helped her choose the gifts. The only place to buy things was the general store, where they sold newspapers and cigarettes and food that could stand on the shelves for a year without rotting. They chose key rings for the children, one each, and for the parents a jar of some pickle Kurt said was the right thing to offer no matter what it tasted like, because it was a speciality of the region.

'Of course I did,' she said.

'And the children? How are they?'

She hadn't really paid much attention to the children. She felt like a child herself. During dinner she couldn't eat or speak. They sat around the table, the father and the mother, the two children and her. They felt, the two girls, a little like rivals; dimly she saw them across the table, two beings competing with her for the evening's resources, almost for consciousness itself. Something was happening to her, to her, yet everyone seemed to think something was happening to them too. The woman kept petting the younger girl and putting her on her lap. When they had finished eating the woman got up to clear the plates. Sonia hesitated and then she got up too and began carrying things to the sink. The woman seemed pleased. Oh thank you, she said.

'They're OK,' she said to Kurt. She told him she had helped with the dishes.

'Good,' he said. 'That's good. Remember you're there to help. You'll get used to being there. It's difficult at first. Everything will seem strange. You'll feel homesick.'

She did not say, did not say that what sickened her was, in fact, the thought of home. The paralysing terror she felt was the opposite of homesickness. It came from her sense that there might be nothing else for her, that she had come out into the world and met its strangeness and indifference like a fist in her face.

'It will all seem better tomorrow,' Kurt said. 'I'll call you again in the evening on my break, same time.'

Kurt was working for the summer in a chicken factory. He worked nights because the pay was better. On his part of the line they took out the chicken's insides, sealed them in a little plastic bag to preserve them, and put them back in the chicken again. Like education, Sonia said. She lay on her bed, darkness at the window, the metal phone hot against her ear. She had failed her English certificate and couldn't complete her college course without it: it was Kurt's suggestion, to defer her place and come here. You can live for free, he said. You live with a family, you help them around the house, and you come back speaking English. She didn't say: if I spoke English I wouldn't come back at all.

'All right,' she said. She didn't ask him anything about himself. She had two pills in her purse she was going to take in a minute, to make her sleep. 'Bye.'

•

The house is big. There are rooms with no one in them, full of paintings and old furniture like a museum. She looks through the doorways but doesn't go in. She goes downstairs and straight out to the garden, to smoke.

Later she leaves the house and walks around the town. The woman has taken the children to school. She says one day Sonia can take them, but for now she'll do it herself. Sonia understands better when the woman speaks than the man. Yet the woman talks about things that don't exist. There's something that comes from her, something other than words. It's as if she isn't contained in her own skin. She spills out and Sonia can see the spillage. She can see what is meant as well as hear it. The woman talks about the future and the past but what she wants right now isn't obvious. So Sonia goes out and walks around.

In the town centre there are so many shops they make a kind of noise. There's a feeling of crisis, almost of panic here: the plate-glass doors stand open, loud music plays, the pavements are swarming with people. The shops are huge inside, like caves, and she stands at their mouths, being shoved by passersby. She watches the customers moving around the aisles, rifling and discarding with the unselfconsciousness of looters. There are long queues at the tills. She doesn't know whether what she is seeing is poverty or luxury.

She goes to look at the sea. The beach is quieter. There are people walking their dogs. The water is grey and fretted by wind. She sits on the shingle, smoking. A man approaches her, a young skinny man in black trousers and a black T-shirt with a picture of a wolf on it. He asks her for a cigarette. They talk for a while. She is surprised that when she says English words they work and he understands. He sits quite close to her on the shingle and stares into her face while she talks. He seems to be interested in her: the feeling is uncomfortable, like a needle probing at a vein. His face is pale; his eyes are green, with long black lashes. She tells him a bit about her family, her home town. Then he mentions that he comes from Lithuania and immediately she wants to get up and leave. She thought he was English, but now she knows his interest is the interest of a lost boy, someone alone who saw her aloneness as if it had been written across her face.

On the way home she passes a little shop hidden in a side street whose window is all decorated with strange pictures, brooding flowers with black outlines, roses shedding drops of blood, daggers with snakes twined around their blades. It is a tattoo parlour. She stands for a long time looking at the window. Then she goes back to the house.

•

Sonia, the woman says, I really need you. Sonia understands that part of the sentence: the words are the words of the American song they play in the bars at home. The rest is harder to make sense of. The woman wants her to go shopping. She writes a list. She draws a map, with a big cross on it for the supermarket. She gives her money, large notes with a thread of silver running through them.

Sonia spends a long time in the supermarket. The supermarket is nice: she feels happy there. She looks at the food. She wanders the aisles, caressing things. At home she does the shopping for her mother. The supermarket is a long way from her mother's house and she has to bring the bags back on the bus. She carries the bags into the kitchen, where her mother and her mother's boyfriend are usually sitting smoking and drinking coffee. They don't thank her; they barely even look at her.

But the woman thanks her. She seems overjoyed. Well done, she says. Well done. Did you get lost? She taps the watch on her wrist, shows the time to Sonia. Sonia has been away for three hours. I was worried, the woman says. I was worried you'd got lost.

She goes to her room and lies on the bed. She bought a package of brownies at the supermarket and she eats them lying there. There are so many that she can eat them without worrying the pleasure will come to an end, but all at once it does and the package is empty. It starts to get dark. She doesn't turn on the lights. She feels sleepy. She lies there, drifting, in her clothes. When the knock at the door comes she is startled; she must have fallen asleep. The woman calls her name through the door. Sonia gets up, her head thick. Yes? she says through the door. The English word comes so strangely from her mouth. The woman asks her if she can come downstairs. I need you, she says.

•

The two little girls don't talk to her and she doesn't talk to them either. She sits on a chair in the corner while they do whatever it is they do. She reads a magazine. When they fight it is harder to concentrate on reading. The magazine is in English. The words are like little pieces of grit in her eyes.

The woman keeps coming into the room and going out again. She seems to be looking for something. There are frown lines on her face. The children put out their arms as she passes, like drowning people. Sonia, she says. Sonia.

In the evening she hears the man and the woman talking. Their conversation never stops. She wonders how they could possibly have so much to say to one another. And in English, too – she knows that isn't a problem for them, but it makes her feel tired. She has started to take three pills at night instead of two. All day she is exhausted and then at night she is flung about in a whirling kind of chaos, all the lights on in her head, spinning and spinning in the splintered darkness. Kurt says her mind is having trouble processing all this new information. He says it will pass. He asks if she's thinking in English yet.

•

The woman isn't pleased with her any more.

Sonia, she says, we need to have a talk.

Maybe later, Sonia says.

It is first thing in the morning and her head is so stuffy with pills she can barely see the coffee grains she is trying to spoon into her cup.

I'm taking the children to school, the woman says. There is the sound of broken glass in her voice. When I come back I want to talk.

Sonia sits at the kitchen table in her pyjamas, waiting. She has found an over-sized cup in one of the cupboards and that is what she makes her coffee in. It is as big as a bowl. She fills it right to the top, the hot milk frothy and sweet, just a few coffee grains stirred in. It takes her a long time to drink it. Sometimes, when she's finished, she makes another one and takes it back to the table. The kitchen is a nice room and she likes to sit here, drinking coffee. A whole morning can pass like that.

The woman returns. She is frowning. She says, you have to get dressed in the mornings. You have to get up and dressed.

I'm tired, Sonia says.

I want you up and dressed and downstairs by eight o'clock in the morning, she says. I want you to help me.

Sonia says nothing.

You need to make friends with the children, she says. It's not up to them. It's up to you.

Sonia says nothing.

I want you to cook, the woman says. I want you to cook dinner. I want you to do the laundry. I want you to tidy up around here.

Sonia stares at her. Her eyes feel very wide open. She can't close them or look away.

You need to do these things, the woman says, or you're going to have to go home.

•

The man goes away. The woman says he will be gone for a week. In the evening Sonia sees her through a crack in the sitting-room door. She sits alone, smoking and staring into space.

Sonia takes four pills and in the morning is woken by the sound of banging on her bedroom door. She is too far away to answer. She can hear gulls screaming somewhere outside. She drifts back into a black-edged sleep. Later, the banging starts again.

Yes, she says hoarsely.

Get up, the woman says through the door. Get up now. Downstairs Sonia finds her in the kitchen, washing the floor with a mop. She plunges the mop in the bucket and bangs it against the floor.

She chases it into the corners. She is all hard angles and frowning lines. For the first time since she came here Sonia sees something she recognises: anger.

What's wrong with you? the woman says. Why can't you get up?

Pills. I take some pills, Sonia says.

What pills?

From the doctor. They make me tired.

What are they for? Why does the doctor give you pills?

I stayed in hospital, Sonia says. It was a long time ago.

Why were you in hospital?

Sonia stares at her wide-eyed. She feels suddenly soft, against this hard anger. She feels relieved.

I hurt myself, she says.

On purpose?

Sonia is silent. She wants to smile, to laugh, to dance, but she feels so beautifully soft that all she can do is yield. She gives a little nod.

How long were you there for? In the hospital?

One year, Sonia says. My sixteen year.

OK, the woman says, shaking her head. OK.

The man had entered her compartment on the train. She was going away to boarding school because her mother said she couldn't be at home any more. At this school you slept and ate your meals, and that was where she was going. The man talked to her while darkness fell outside the windows of the speeding carriage, wadding the flat wastes like a kind of black fog through which the spectral forms of darkened factories sometimes loomed and then vanished. He reminded her of her father, with his steel-framed glasses and his hair with bits of grey in it. He locked the carriage door and he took her long ponytail in his hand and twisted it through his fingers. Then he yanked it so hard she thought her neck would break.

I should have been told this, the woman says. Her arms are folded tight against her chest. She stares out of the window at the garden. Don't you think I should have been told this?

The man went to prison eventually. Her mother said it was a terrible thing, to ruin a man's life. She said Sonia must have provoked him. So one evening Sonia cut her wrists, and her arms too for good measure. She was put in a psychiatric hospital: that was where she met Kurt.

I'm going to have to phone the agency, the woman says. I'm sorry, but you're going to have to go home.

I can't go home, Sonia says. I have nowhere to go.

I'm sorry, the woman says again. She looks at her watch. God, I'm late, she says. I've got to pick up the children and I'm going to be late.

She rushes away and Sonia hears the front door close. After a while she goes outside to smoke a cigarette. The sky is iron-grey and heavy. A gust of wind makes the door to the kitchen slam. While she smokes a kind of darkness seems to gather over the garden, to tower over it, growing and leaning like a black cliff. She puts out her cigarette. The rain comes hard and fast. It's only a few paces back to the house from the garden but by the time she gets in she is wet.

A little while later she hears the front door open, the sounds of footsteps and voices in the hall. Sonia comes out of her room. The woman stands in the hall with the two children. Water drips from them on to the hall floor. The woman wears only a T-shirt: it is so wet that Sonia can see her skin through it. She sees that the younger

child is wearing the woman's coat; the older one has her umbrella.
Water runs from the woman's hair. She is shaking so violently that
Sonia can hear her teeth knocking together. She tries to speak.

I, she says. I.

Then, very slowly, her body racked by tremors, she begins to
climb the stairs, leaving a trail of water behind her. She passes Sonia
without speaking on the landing. The children are still standing,
staring up at her, in the hall. She goes into her bedroom and closes
the door.

•

Sonia makes the noodles in cream sauce that her grandmother used
to make for her when she was small. Her grandmother lived in a big
house in the countryside and Sonia would spend the school holidays
there. Sonia loved her grandmother. She puts lots of grated cheese
on top of the noodles. She is frightened they won't like it but the
children eat it all.

The woman does not come down. After dinner Sonia goes up
and knocks at her door. There is no reply. After a while she opens
the door a little. The woman is lying in bed, asleep. Her tangled
hair spread over the pillow is still damp. Sonia takes the children
upstairs and runs the bath for them. She finds their pyjamas in
their rooms. When they try to go into their mother's room she stops
them. Mummy's sleeping, she says. At midnight she looks in again.
The woman is exactly as she was, sleeping, except that the covers
are pushed back. She is still wearing the clothes she got wet in.

Sonia sets the alarm on her phone to wake her up in the morning. She is about to take her pills and then she doesn't. Before break-

fast, when she looks in, the woman's eyes are open. The whites are yellow. She tries to speak. Water, she says. Sonia gets a jug of water and a glass and puts them beside her bed. The woman gets up on her elbow to drink. The glass shakes violently in her hand and the water spills. She falls back against the pillows. She tries to say something but her eyes keep closing. Sonia goes downstairs, where the children are waiting for her. The younger one asks her to brush her hair. Sonia brushes it and then she braids it smoothly into a high plait. The little girl goes to look at herself in the mirror and when she comes back she seems pleased.

They show her the way to school. At the gate Sonia isn't sure what to do. Then she gives each of them an awkward little hug and they run off into the playground.

•

The man calls. Sonia tells him the woman is ill. Oh dear, he says. He asks her if she can manage on her own. Of course, she says. That's great, he says. It's difficult for me to come back. That's a real help.

The woman lies in bed for hour after hour. Sometimes she can speak and sometimes she can't. The children, she says. Occasionally Sonia notices that the bed is completely soaked. The woman has a fever. Sonia brings her water. Kurt calls and she describes the woman's symptoms. Pneumonia, he says confidently. When the children return from school they ask to see her. She replies that Mummy's ill and needs to be left alone. She makes gingerbread for them, with a special cream-cheese icing. They want to stir the mixture and she lets them. The next day, when they are at school, she walks around the town. She goes to the supermarket and chooses what she likes.

She goes to the shops and looks at the clothes. She passes the tattoo parlour. She stands outside it, looking at the pictures on the windows. Then, after a while, she opens the door and goes in.

The man behind the counter is reading a newspaper. He has big hoops in his ears. She stares at them so as not to stare at the rest of him. His skin is like jungle, like ivy. The patterns swarm all the way up his throat. He shows her pictures in a book. He says, once you've done this you can't change your mind, you know that don't you? She chooses a rose, just one. Where? he says. She bares her shoulder. She is careful not to let her sleeves slip down. She doesn't want him to see the scars on her arms. While he works he talks but she doesn't understand what he says. He doesn't hurt her much.

•

She buys a book for the little girls, a children's book in her own language. She teaches them a few words. She points at things and says the name in her own tongue, and they repeat after her. When she goes in to give the woman her water, she finds her sitting up in bed for the first time. Her face is bloodless and white. Her hair is matted. The room has a strange smell.

Where are the children, she says.

With me, Sonia says. They are with me.

Tell them to come up, she says. I want to see them.

Maybe later, Sonia says. We are cooking just now. You need to rest.

The man is coming back. She has cleaned the house. She has made everything look nice. She is cooking a special meal, mushrooms in cream sauce, fried onions, potatoes with melted cheese, and the children are helping her cook. The younger girl hurts her finger on the metal grater when she is grating the cheese for Sonia. She cries. She says she wants to see her mother. The sobs go through her in big shudders. Sonia finds her a plaster and wraps it around the finger. She gives her a piece of gingerbread. She takes her on her lap, as she has seen the woman do, and to her surprise the little girl lets her.

Well done, the man says when he comes back. He looks around at the tidy house, at the kitchen full of good smells. Well done. I don't know what we'd have done without you.

He hugs the children. He goes up to see the woman but soon comes back down again. He says she is asleep. He says he is starving hungry. They sit around the table, the four of them, eating her food. Just as they are finishing a sound comes from upstairs. It is the sound of footsteps. The footsteps are slow; sometimes they stop and then start again. After a while the woman appears in the doorway. She is wearing a crumpled nightdress. Her hair stands up in a shock. Her lips are a bluish colour. She is very white, and much thinner than she was before. She puts her hand against the doorway for support. She looks at them all sitting there. She tries to smile.

Hello, she says.

•

Sonia doesn't speak to Kurt so much any more. When he calls, she sees the number flashing and decides not to answer. She is too busy to talk to him. She has made some new friends and often in the evenings they go out. They go to bars and clubs; they go dancing. Sonia has bought a new top, backless, to show off her tattoo. People compliment her on it so often that she goes back to the tattoo par-

lour and gets another one, a long flowering bramble that twists all
the way down her spine.

She takes the children to school in the mornings and in the afternoon she picks them up again. On the way they hold her hands.
They sit in the kitchen making things, pumpkin cupcakes, strudel,
the things she used to make with her grandmother. She had forgotten these things until now. When Christmas comes she makes a
felt calendar with them, like the ones she used to have. She sews
the pockets, one for each day, and puts a chocolate in each one. The
children help her hang it on the wall. Look, they say to the man.
Look what Sonia made us. Well done Sonia, he says. Well done.

The woman stays in her room. Sometimes she comes and stands
in the kitchen doorway. She doesn't seem to know what to do. She
looks at Sonia and the children and she goes away again. These days
it is the man Sonia takes her orders from. He writes the shopping
lists. He teaches her to cook some English dishes. She understands
that her food is too heavy; she learns to cook things that are more
refined. One day he asks her what she is doing and she tells him
she is making the herb marinade for the chicken. He laughs. You're
a fast learner, he says. He tells her how much her English has improved. He corrects her mistakes.

At Christmas they buy her a present, a white woollen coat that
buttons up tight around her body. She has given them a large stollen she baked herself. She phoned up her grandmother and asked
for the recipe. When they unwrapped it they all clapped and ex-
claimed. She has never worn anything like the white coat before.
They watch her try it on. The woman says, it looks lovely Sonia.
She is sitting in the corner, biting her nails. Sonia can tell from the
expression on her face that the woman chose the coat herself. She

thanks her. Later she puts it in a bag under her bed, and pushes it as far into the darkness as she can.

•

The man has moved into a different bedroom. Sonia sees his things there when she goes in to clean. The woman spends all her time in the room they used to share. She comes down at mealtimes and sits silently at the table. She doesn't eat the food Sonia has cooked.

Things are a bit difficult at the moment, the man tells her. You're being a real help. Well done.

Sometimes she hears them shouting at each other. They stay up until late at night. During the day she hears the woman crying in her room. In the evenings, when they've finally gone to bed, Sonia goes down to the kitchen to eat cereal. Her body has started to crave starch. The food they eat is all protein, and she misses the comforting feeling of blandness filling her mouth. Sometimes she will eat a whole box, saturating the bowl to the top with milk. Where's all the milk gone? the woman will say, angrily, in the morning.

One evening she finds the woman in the kitchen alone. She is smoking and staring out of the window. Oh hello Sonia, she says.

Can I smoke too? Sonia says.

Go ahead, the woman says, waving her hand to show that she doesn't care.

They sit there and smoke in silence. Then the woman starts to ask her about her family. She asks about her father, her mother, about where they live.

My parents divorced, Sonia says. They live far apart from each other.

How old were you? the woman asks.

Ten I think, Sonia says.

And who did you live with? the woman says. Your mother or your father?

I wanted to live with my father, Sonia says. But his new wife didn't like it.

What about your mother? the woman says.

She didn't want me there. She doesn't like me. I stayed a lot of the time with my grandmother. My mother doesn't like my grandmother either. She ran away from home when she was sixteen. She ran away with my father.

The woman raises her eyebrows. She has a stricken expression on her face. How old was your mother when you were born? she says.

She was already pregnant with me when she ran away, Sonia says. She was sixteen.

So she's the same age now as me, the woman says.

Younger than you, Sonia says.

I want to say, the woman says after a pause, I want to say that I'm sorry these things have happened to you. I'm really sorry.

Sonia gazes at her. Her head swims with a warm liquid feeling. She feels soft suddenly, soft as dough.

Someone should apologise to you, the woman says. So that's what I'm doing. I'm saying sorry.

She gets up and before she leaves the room she comes and gives Sonia a hug. Her body is hard and bony. Sonia can still feel the imprint of it on her own soft flesh long after she's gone.

•

The man says, Sonia I need you.

He is packing his things. He wants her to help him. He tells her what to do. She fills boxes and folds clothes neatly into suitcases. She smoothes her hands over the folded shirts and aligns the tightly paired socks.

In the evening Kurt calls.

At last I've saved the money for a ticket, he says. I'm coming to visit you.

She thinks about it.

Let's meet in London, she says. I want to see Buckingham Palace and Big Ben. I want to go to some clubs.

OK, Kurt says admiringly. It's easier for me, anyhow.

I know somewhere cheap we can stay, she says.

They stay in a hostel in Leicester Square, the two of them crammed into a single bed. She and Kurt have never made love. He has never asked her to. They stay out at a club all night and then sleep all day.

My next job will be in London, Sonia says. London is a great city.

He asks about the family she lives with.

They're great, she says.

And the children?

The children are really cute, she says.

She shows him pictures she's taken of them on her phone.

•

When she gets back the man has gone. His room is empty. It is raining outside; she watches the rain for a while through the windows of his empty room. Later he phones her and asks her to bring the children round to his new house after school. She cooks dinner for them all in the unfamiliar kitchen. She goes back to the other house to sleep: there isn't enough room for her to sleep at the man's house. She doesn't see the woman, though she hears her walking around during the night.

The next day she takes the children to the man's new house again. Towards evening the woman rings the bell. The older girl goes to let her in. Sonia and the man are sitting around the table having dinner. The younger girl is sitting on Sonia's lap. Sonia has plaited her hair.

The woman comes in and stares at them. She looks at Sonia. Her face is shocked. She and the man go off somewhere to talk. Then she goes away again, taking the children with her. Before they go, they hug Sonia. They cling to her. Be good girls, she says to them. Go with your mummy.

She and the man are left alone. She clears the dishes and tidies up. Eventually he tells her she can go. I don't need you for anything else, he says.

At home, the woman is waiting for her in the hall.

I want you to leave, she says. You can't stay here any more.

Sonia looks at her with wide-open eyes.

There's no job for you any more, the woman says. I'm sorry.

Sonia has trouble recognising the woman's power to make this decision. Surely it's up to the man too?

There's no job for you there either, the woman says. Then she adds, We have to do this ourselves.

Sonia thinks she will find out about that in private. She has the man's number on her mobile phone. He calls her all the time with instructions. He needs her.

Believe me, the woman says. Believe me, that isn't going to work.

The woman looks terrible. She is so thin she looks like a skeleton. One side of her face is swollen and she keeps her hand there, holding it over her cheek.

They pulled out my tooth, she says. It still hurts where they pulled it out.

Where will I go? Sonia says.

The woman swallows, closes her eyes, presses her hand to her cheek.

I've found you a job with another family, she says. In London.

For a moment a kind of chasm seems to open up beside her, disclosing a vast grey cityscape where the walls of the house ought to be. Sonia is frightened. She wants to run to her room and lock herself inside. She wants to crawl under the bed and hide there.

No, she says. No I don't want.

She can't speak. They stand there face to face in the electric light of the hall. The woman's face is anguished, ugly. She stands at the foot of the stairs, as though barring Sonia's way up. She is expelling her.

It's all right, the woman says then, taking her hand from her cheek and resting it on Sonia's arm. It's my sister's family. You met her once, remember? She knows all about you. She's happy to have you. It's the least we can do, she says, and she closes her eyes again.

•

London is great. London is a great city. At the new place Sonia has her own separate flat on the lower floor of the family's house. She joins a gym. She's out almost every night. There are four children here instead of two, but there is less work because the new woman likes to do most things for them herself.

At Christmas she thinks of the old family. Something makes her think of them. It is winter now, and darkness falls at four o'clock. Sonia walks in her new coat, a fake fur she bought for herself on Oxford Street. She is walking home through the residential streets of her neighbourhood. It is a wealthy neighbourhood, all family houses with clipped hedges and neat front gardens. The lights are on inside and as she passes she looks through the windows, looks at the people in their warm bright rooms. And she remembers then how she left the old house; how the woman had called her a taxi to the train station, how they said goodbye on the front step. The woman went back inside and closed the door. Sonia carried her suitcase alone to the taxi, but before she got in she looked back, back at the house whose windows were all dark; and she saw, dimly, the shape of the woman inside, saw her sitting there alone in the darkness.

When she gets home she finds her grandmother's recipe and she makes a big stollen in the kitchenette of her flat. It takes her all evening and half the night. The little room gets so hot she has to open the windows and let the freezing air in. She takes off her sweater and works in her vest, her arms bare. When it's cooked and cooled she takes a long sharp knife and she cuts it carefully into two equal pieces, and she wraps each piece in muslin and then in foil and then in bright Christmas paper, and she puts the pieces in two boxes to post in the morning, one to the man and one to the woman.

ACKNOWLEDGEMENTS

Certain people made it possible for me to write this book and I would like to thank them. My sister Sarah has been my mainstay and friend: for the past year not just her time but also her gift for happiness and family life have been on semi-permanent loan to my household. Russell Celyn Jones has lived through and been instrumental in the creation of these chapters; to him I owe, among so many other things, the notion of aftermath that is the book's elemental theme. Hannah Griffiths remained endlessly faithful to the feminist principle of autobiographical writing, even when it hurt. Andrew Wylie and Sarah Chalfant continued to treat me as a writer until eventually I became one again. David Rogers, Meg Jensen and Adam Baron of Kingston University were generous colleagues as well as good friends. My parents have been tirelessly supportive, and at a crucial moment provided me with time to write. And thank you most of all to my fine daughters, Albertine and Jessye, who have endured hard times with such dignity and fortitude. It is impossible to meet them and not feel cheered by their triumph over sadness. I am prouder of them than I can say; I hope one day they will read this and feel, at least, not ashamed.